Creating the Child-centred Classroom

Susan Schwartz

Mindy Pollishuke

Richard C. Owen Publishers, Inc.

Katonah, New York

Copyright © 1991 by Richard C. Owen Publishers, Inc.
Copyright © 1990 by Irwin Publishing.
Published by arrangement with Stoddart Publishing Co.
Limited, Toronto, Ontario, Canada.

Library of Congress Cataloging-in-Publication Data

Schwartz, Susan, 1951-
Creating the child-centred classroom/Susan Schwartz, Mindy Pollishuke.
p.   cm.
Reprint. Originally published: Toronto, Canada: Irwin Pub., 1989.
Includes bibliographical references (p.   ).
ISBN 1-878450-14-X
1. Language experience approach in education. 2. Activity programs in education. 3. Inter-disciplinary approach in education. 4. Classroom environment. I. Pollishuke, Mindy, 1951-
II. Title.
LB1576.S327   1991
372.13—dc20   90-26326
                                                                                                              CIP

Front cover photo: Gabe Palmer, © Palmer/Kane, Inc. 1978/Masterfile
Text and Cover Design by Julian Cleva
Illustrations by Julian Cleva
Photographs by Barry Griffiths/Network Stock Photo
Typesetting by Jay Tee Graphics

Published by
Richard C. Owen Publishers, Inc.
PO Box 585
Katonah, New York 10536

Printed in the United States of America
9 8 7 6 5

Contents

Introduction 1

1. Whole Language and Active Learning: A Philosophical Model 2
Creating an Understanding 2

2. The Physical Set-up of the Classroom 9
Creating the Physical Set-up of the Classroom 9

3. Timetabling 13
Creating Timetabling Possibilities 13

4. Classroom Atmosphere 18
Creating an Effective Learning Atmosphere 19

5. Whole Language 28
i) Creating a Language-rich Environment 28
ii) Creating Reflective Speaking Experiences 30
iii) Creating Active Listening Experiences 31
iv) Creating Focussed Viewing Experiences 32
v) Creating Reflective Dramatizing Experiences 33
vi) Creating Meaningful Reading Experiences 34
vii) Creating Purposeful Writing Experiences 41

6. An Integrated Child-centred Curriculum 49
Creating an Integrated Child-centred Curriculum 50

7. Learning Centres 56
Creating Effective Learning Centres 57

8. Record Keeping, Student Evaluation and Parental Involvement 76
i) Creating Effective Record-keeping and Student Evaluation Practices 77
ii) Creating and Improving Parental Involvement 85

Conclusion 94

Appendix: Favourite Children's Books 95

Bibliography 98

Blackline Masters 100
For Student Use 101
BL 1 Student Evaluation Sheet 102
BL 2 Student Evaluation Sheet 103
BL 3 Student Contract 104
BL 4 Student Contract 105
BL 5 Student Reading Record Sheet 106
BL 6 Student Writing Record Sheet 107
BL 7 Student Planning Sheet 106
BL 8-BL 13 Student Tracking Sheets 109-114

For Teacher Use 115
BL 14 Teacher Procedure Planning Sheet 116
BL 15 Teacher Learning Centre Checklist 118
BL 16 Teacher Learning Centre Checklist 119
BL 17 Teacher Learning Centre Checklist 120
BL 18 Teacher Planning Sheet 121
BL 19 Teacher Long-range Planning Sheet 122
BL 20 Teacher Observation Sheet 123
BL 21 Teacher Observation Summary Sheet 124
BL 22 Teacher Checklist for Completed Activities 125
BL 23 Teacher Checklist for Writing 126
BL 24 Teacher Writing Conference Sheet 127
BL 25 Teacher Parent/Guardian Interview Checklist 128

Sample Letters to Parents/Guardians 129
BL 26-BL 32 Parent/Guardian Letters 130-137

Acknowledgements

Just as all of us are products of our experiences and our environment, we, as authors, are products of the North York system. Educated, trained and employed by the North York Board of Education, our ideas and beliefs cannot help but be influenced and shaped by North York philosophies and values. We therefore wish to thank the North York Board of Education for allowing and encouraging us to expand our knowledge, to learn from our experiences and to grow as professionals and individuals. We also wish to thank North York for allowing us to use and refer to its documents and guidelines.

Special appreciation and thanks to:

- Shirley Stanton, Assistant Superintendent of Westview Family of Schools, North York Board, for her continued encouragement and support;
- Elizabeth Hartman, teacher in the North York Board of Education, for her dedication and commitment to the child-centred classroom;
- our colleagues in North York for their friendship, support and expertise;
- the students of Firgrove Public School for their active participation in the child-centred classroom;
- Brigitte Brennan, Eileen Gold, Tamara Quinton, and Barbara Singer, teachers in York Region Board of Education, for sharing their ideas regarding learning centres and tracking sheets;

and

- to our husbands, Saul and Stephen; our children, Marnie, Rena, Michael, Kimberly and Matthew; and our family and friends; we give a warm and loving thanks for encouraging us and allowing us the time and opportunity to work freely on this book.

Introduction

In the Child-centred Classroom

Children	Teacher	Atmosphere
Deciding, discovering,	Moving and modelling,	Fostering, freeing,
Challenging, creating,	Instructing, involving,	Stirring and stimulating,
Seeking and sharing:	Chatting and caring:	Inspiring, encouraging:
Risk-taking.	**Facilitating.**	**Liberating.**

(Courtesy of Sharon Stewart, Toronto, Canada)

If you have picked up this book, you may be asking yourself, "What is a child-centred classroom, and what would I see if I walked into one?" The above poem serves as a "snapshot" of the ideal situation, but a snapshot is not enough. It illustrates *some* of the features of the child-centred classroom, but it leaves many unanswered questions such as:

- What is active learning?
- How do I integrate the curriculum?
- How do I meet the needs of all of my students?
- How do I create a child-centred classroom?
- Where do I begin?

As educational program consultants, we are often asked these questions. This book is our attempt to answer them. We provide many practical implementation strategies along with a clear outline of the theory behind the child-centred classroom — a theory which, in our opinion, involves an understanding of the concepts of whole language and active learning.

We believe that theory and practice go hand in hand. Therefore, we hope you will use the ideas in this book to build your own beliefs and understandings, and to develop your own philosophy regarding the child-centred classroom. Once you have an understanding, you can begin to effectively implement child-centred strategies. You will bring your own learning style, your own life experiences and your own unique feelings into the classroom. You will bring all available information and resources together, some old, some new, to create a classroom that is truly your own.

We hope you will use the many practical classroom strategies that we suggest as a base from which to begin, a springboard from which to experiment, to modify and to adapt to fit your own and your students' individual needs and strengths.

Although there are many references to planning and implementation in all curriculum areas, we do not intend our suggestions to form a comprehensive guide for all subjects. Rather, we hope you will consider our recommended activities as a sampling of possibilities that you might find helpful. Whether you are new to the profession or simply interested in change, we hope you will find our ideas informative, practical, innovative and, above all else, exciting!

1

Whole Language and Active Learning: A Philosophical Model

What is whole language? What is active learning? Both of these terms reflect a belief in how children learn. Children learn in natural situations where they are actively investigating the world around them. Through their interactions with others, they learn to use language to make their experiences meaningful and to communicate their understandings. They communicate by listening, speaking, reading and writing. These are the components of language, but whole language views these components as interrelated, interwoven with all parts equally important.

Whole language also views the learning of language as a *whole* experience rather than as a fragmented one. Letters, sounds and words are not really language until they are put together to form whole and meaningful thoughts or ideas.

In the following section, you will see the interrelationships that exist between all the components of language and all the elements of active learning. You will also see how the two fit together to create the child-centred classroom. For the purposes of clarification, each component is discussed separately.

Creating an Understanding

Children learn to read by interacting with the *whole*, the whole story, the whole poem, the whole experience. They begin to view themselves as readers as they look closely at books and notice the print in the environment around them. They attach meaning and build relationships between print and the spoken word.

In a whole language classroom, children are *read to often* and develop a positive attitude towards reading and books. Children *read often*, always for meaning and for enjoyment. They *speak* about their reading, they *listen to* others read and speak, they *write* about what they have read in order to share their own understandings, and they *read* what they *write*. All the components of language are interconnected (Fig. 1.1).

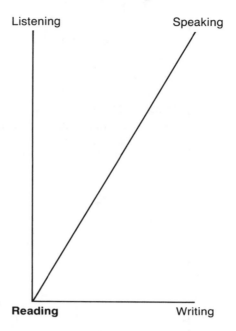

Figure 1.1

Similarly, in a whole language classroom, children *write often*. They *speak* to clarify their ideas for their writing, they *listen* to others read and speak, they *read* to get ideas for their writing, they *write* for a purpose—to convey meaning—they respond to questions about their writing and they *read* what they *write*. Again, all the components of language are seen to be interrelated, and writing is seen as a meaningful, ongoing, interactive process (Fig. 1.2).

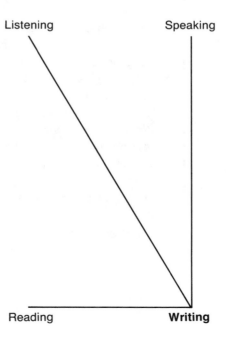

Figure 1.2

Traditionally the listening and speaking aspects of language have not been emphasized enough in the classroom. Reading and writing have always been the focus of any language arts program. The listening and speaking, or oral components, were included on an incidental basis only. Children were *expected* to listen—mainly to the teacher—and were given little opportunity to speak, to clarify their thoughts, or to discuss their ideas with peers.

In the whole language classroom, *listening* and *speaking* are essential components (Fig. 1.3). *Talk*, the integration of *listening* and *speaking*, allows children opportunities to gain knowledge, to explore, clarify and rehearse their ideas. They *talk* about their experiences and their innermost thoughts and feelings. They *talk* about their *writing*, before, during and after composing. They *listen* to good reading models often and *talk* about their *reading* and *writing* experiences. They have frequent opportunities to interact with peers and adults, to communicate often in meaningful situations.

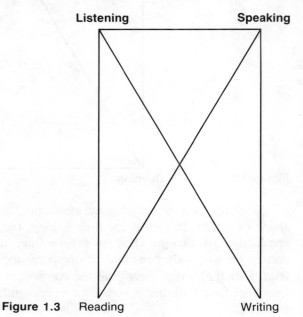

Figure 1.3   Listening   Speaking   Reading   Writing

In a whole language classroom, it would be difficult to see where the reading program ends and the writing program begins. Listening and speaking opportunities are interwoven throughout as children participate in *reading*, *writing*, *listening*, and *speaking*. Therefore, these four components of language become *whole* language when they are interwoven, one into the other, in a cyclical pattern, all being given equal emphasis, with meaning as the ultimate goal (Fig. 1.4).

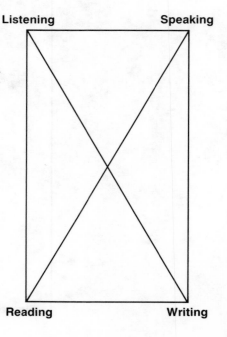

Figure 1.4   Listening   Speaking   Reading   Writing

Our model of whole language also includes *viewing* as a component, defined here as "observing with a focus" (Fig. 1.5). Viewing becomes a part of language when children *talk* about what they see. They *listen* to others share their ideas and responses. They *read* and *write* about their observations. They begin to observe with a new focus and understanding. They become more critical and perceptive in the way they view the world around them.

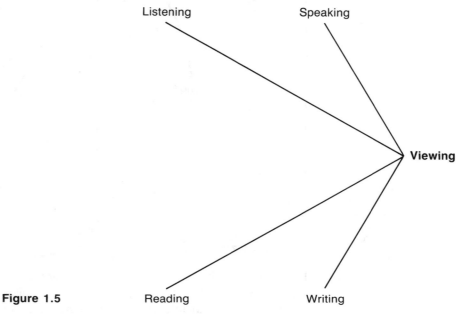

Figure 1.5

Dramatizing, usually considered as an essential component of the Arts, is included here as another important form of communication (Fig. 1.6). Children draw upon and *share* their experiences through role playing. They *read* stories and then bring them to life through storytelling and dramatization. They *listen* and *observe* others in role-playing situations. They *write* about their experiences, and they *read* what they *write*. They *view*, *listen*, *speak*, *read* and *write* about what they observe. Here again, a cyclical, ongoing process is at work.

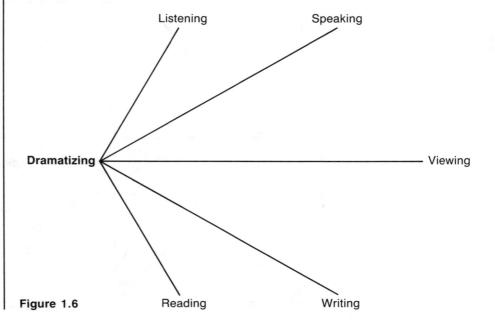

Figure 1.6

A hexagonal shape with all component parts interrelated provides a concrete, visual illustration of whole language (Fig. 1.7).

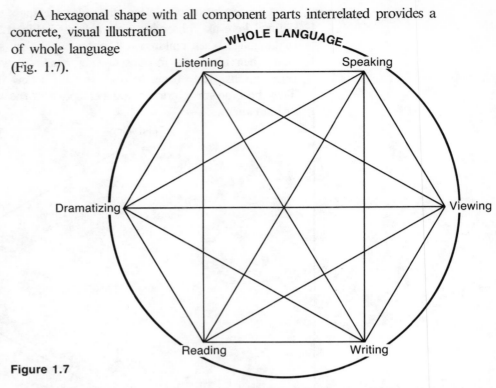

Figure 1.7

Just as the components of *whole language* are interwoven, so too are the elements of *active learning* (Fig. 1.8). Children learn by doing—by experiencing and interacting with people and with varied materials in their environment.

Children engaged in active learning are "experiencing, interacting, reflecting and communicating" (*Active Learning in the Junior Division*, North York Board of Education, p. 10). Children learn when *meaning* and *comprehension* are the ultimate goals. They learn by *reflecting* on their experiences and by sharing and *communicating* with others in countless ways. They learn in purposeful, non-threatening environments.

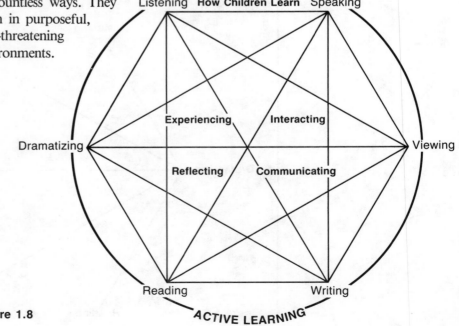

Figure 1.8

Active learning implies active, meaningful language experiences. In a truly active learning environment, children participate in *active* listening, *reflective* speaking, *focussed* viewing, *purposeful* writing, *meaningful* reading, and *reflective* dramatizing (Fig. 1.9).

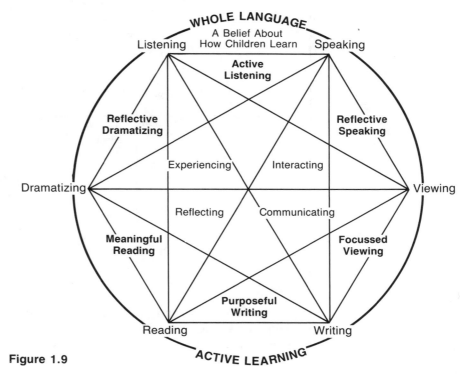

Figure 1.9

As Figure 1.10 (page 8) illustrates, in a whole language, active learning classroom, there is an emphasis on:

- **decision-making** and **problem-solving** opportunities to encourage independent, responsible and critical thinkers
- **integrated learning** as a way of relating a variety of experiences in meaningful ways
- **quality reading material** where children interact with literature in authentic situations
- **real issues or events** that emanate from and have an impact on each individual child
- **talk** to express, clarify and rehearse thoughts and ideas through both active listening and reflective speaking
- **critical observation** to promote more focussed and perceptive observations of the world
- **discovery learning** to encourage a concrete, hands-on approach to learning
- **risk taking** to allow children the freedom to learn *from* and *through* their mistakes
- **learning as a process**, which ultimately results in better performance
- **conferencing** to promote interaction and co-operation with both adults and peers to help clarify and communicate meanings and understandings
- **fluency** in both written and oral expression to develop literate, proficient users of language.

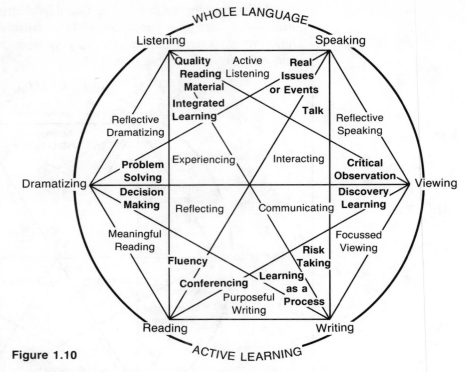

Figure 1.10

Active learning and whole language are essential to the creation of the child-centred classroom. Both language learning and active learning become more meaningful and more purposeful when a teacher provides opportunities that stem from the child's experiences, from the child's own perspective (Fig. 1.11).

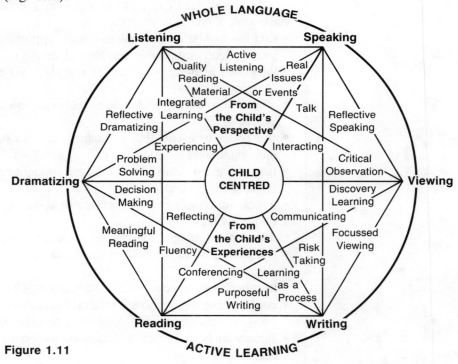

Figure 1.11

The teacher who has this understanding and is able to put these elements into practice will be creating the child-centred classroom!

The Physical Set-up of the Classroom

The classroom environment you create has a profound effect on the social, emotional, physical and intellectual development of the children you teach. To gain a positive attitude towards school and learning, children must have visual stimulation, organization, space and a feeling of warmth and security. Devoting time and energy to the planning and physical set-up of your classroom is well worthwhile.

One of the first things for you to set up in your classroom is a *large group meeting area*, an essential element of the child-centred classroom. Close proximity to the teacher and peers encourages discussion, group interaction and a relaxed flow of ideas.

You might want to set up specific *work areas* in the room to encourage children to share, co-operate and work together. Also, setting up specific areas for art materials and audio-visual equipment may help you use the physical characteristics of your room to their best advantage. Placing a variety of storage facilities around the room, near the work areas, provides children with easy access to resources and materials, and encourages student independence.

A variety of display areas enhances the physical appearance of the child-centred classroom. It also instills pride and ownership and increases motivation to achieve as students see their work on display.

Creating the Physical Set-up of the Classroom

■ Set up a large group meeting area (preferably carpeted).

■ Set up a work area (near the sink if possible) for art, paint and/or craft activities.

■ Set up a work area close to the electrical outlets to facilitate the use of audio-visual equipment (tape recorder, record player, computer, overhead projector, filmstrip projector, etc).

■ Set up the furniture to accommodate small groupings of students working together.

Figure 2.1 shows some furniture arrangements you can try.

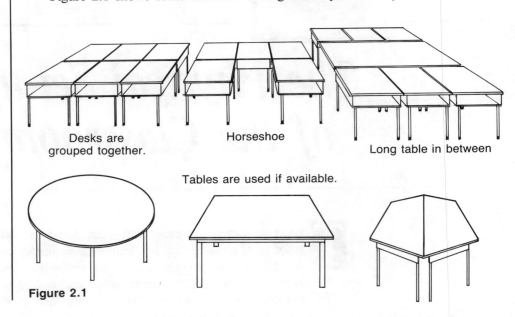

Desks are grouped together.

Horseshoe

Long table in between

Tables are used if available.

Figure 2.1

■ Set up shelves and/or other containers for storage and display of materials and resources. These may be placed near the work areas or around the periphery of the room for easy access by the students.

Figure 2.2 illustrates some arrangements you can use.

Figure 2.2

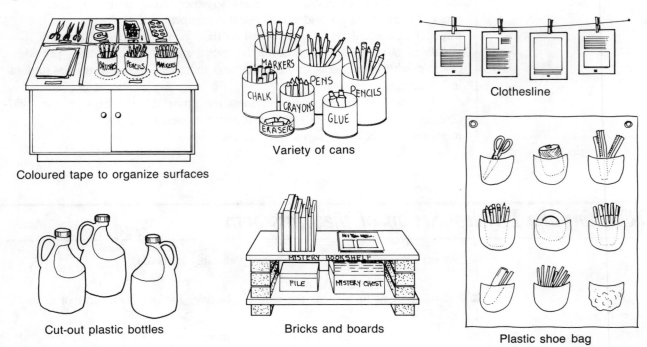

Coloured tape to organize surfaces

Variety of cans

Clothesline

Cut-out plastic bottles

Bricks and boards

Plastic shoe bag

Figure 2.2 continued

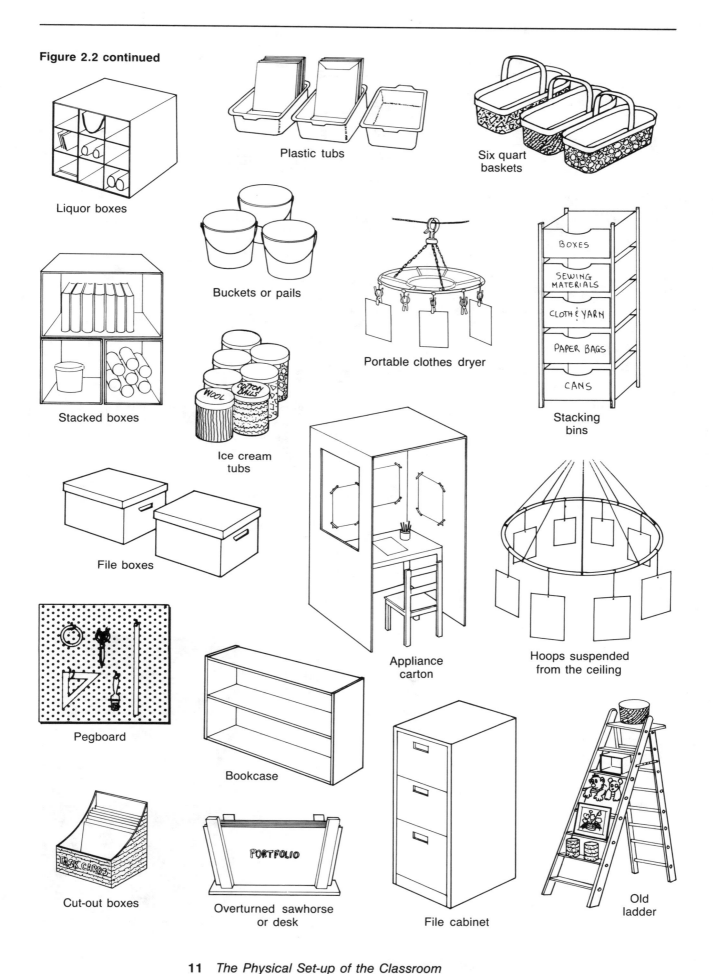

Liquor boxes

Plastic tubs

Six quart baskets

Buckets or pails

Portable clothes dryer

Stacking bins

Stacked boxes

Ice cream tubs

File boxes

BOXES

SEWING MATERIALS

CLOTH & YARN

PAPER BAGS

CANS

WOOL

COTTON BALLS

Appliance carton

Hoops suspended from the ceiling

Pegboard

Bookcase

Cut-out boxes

TASK CARDS

Overturned sawhorse or desk

PORTFOLIO

File cabinet

Old ladder

■ Determine areas for teacher and/or student displays. Be creative!
Figure 2.3 shows some possibilities.

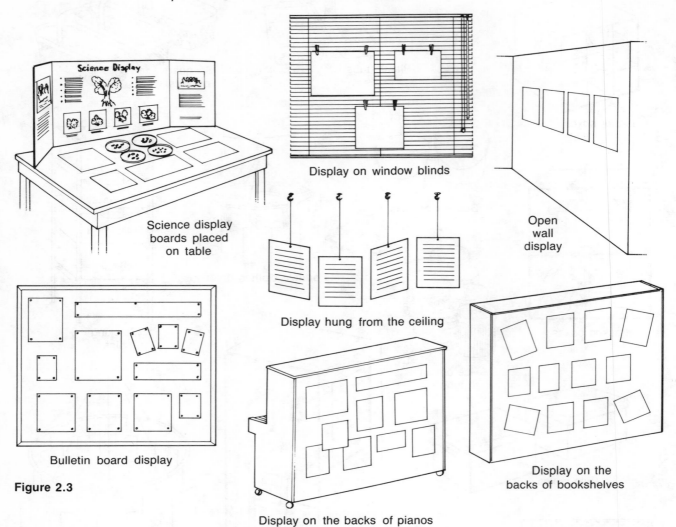

Display on window blinds

Science display boards placed on table

Open wall display

Display hung from the ceiling

Bulletin board display

Figure 2.3

Display on the backs of pianos

Display on the backs of bookshelves

■ Observe your classroom in action and evaluate the overall physical set-up for definition of space, comfort, and organization, and for accessibility of materials and resources (Fig. 2.4).

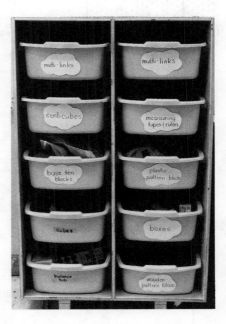

Figure 2.4

Timetabling

You will find that no *one* timetable can accommodate every child's needs, every style of learning or every programming consideration. Learning takes time, and when preparing a timetable, it is important to remember to be flexible—flexible to adapt to children's ever-changing needs and flexible to adjust to changes in planning and programming.

Class scheduling involves planning for *blocks of time. Horizontal* blocks of time, which usually occur at the same time each day, are often necessary to meet school organizational requirements. You may find that times for physical education, or French (which may be taught by someone other than yourself) usually need to be scheduled first. On the other hand, larger *vertical* blocks of time are essential in the child-centred day. They promote longer and more sustained attention to tasks and accommodate more intensive, active investigations. They also provide opportunities for children to pursue their own areas of interest and/or plan collaboratively with you.

When planning your day, try to include daily *input sessions* and regular *sharing times*. Daily input sessions allow time for large group discussion, instruction, explanation and direction; sharing times allow children to celebrate what they know, what they have learned, and what they have accomplished. Their self-concept and confidence improve as they share and take pride in their efforts.

Creating Timetabling Possibilities

■ Examine your timetable and, where necessary, schedule horizontal blocks of time for certain subject areas.

Figure 3.1 (page 14) illustrates horizontal blocks of time.

	Mon.	Tues.	Wed.	Thurs.	Fri.
8:45	Writing	Writing	Writing	Writing	Writing
9:15	Phys. Ed.	Phys. Ed.	Phys. Ed.	Phys. Ed.	Phys. Ed.
9:45	French	French	French	French	French
10:30 11:30					
12:45	D.E.A.R.*	D.E.A.R.	D.E.A.R.	D.E.A.R.	D.E.A.R.
1:15 2:30 3:30					

Figure 3.1

* D.E.A.R. means "Drop Everything and Read."

■ Once these horizontal blocks of time are scheduled, examine your timetable for larger blocks of time.

Figure 3.2 highlights vertical blocks of time.

	Mon.	Tues.	Wed.	Thurs.	Fri.
8:45					
9:15					
9:45					
10:30 11:30	↕	**VERTICAL**	**BLOCKS**		↕
12:45					
1:15 2:30 3:30	↕	**VERTICAL**	**BLOCKS**		↕

Figure 3.2

- Choose some of these vertical blocks to slowly introduce whole-class, co-operative group learning activities. (Refer to Chapter 4). Some of these blocks of time will later be used when students participate in learning centre activities. (Refer to Chapter 7.)

- Allow time for flexible input sessions and time for sharing, interspersed throughout the day when appropriate.

- Expect to make adjustments to your timetable as you grow in your understanding and experiences with co-operative group learning and learning centres.

EXAMPLE 1   If your learning centre time involves student movement by rotation (refer to Chapter 7), the following timetables may prove useful.

A) In a rotation system where students work in one of a possible six centres each day, the rotation cycle will be completed over a six-day period (Fig. 3.3).

A Six-Day Cycle

	Mon.	Tues.	Wed.	Thurs.	Fri.	Mon.	Tues.
10:30-11:30	1st Rotation	2nd Rotation	3rd Rotation	4th Rotation	5th Rotation	6th Rotation	1st Rotation

Figure 3.3

B) Once you and your students become more comfortable with rotations, you may want to participate in *two* centres each day during *two* time blocks. It will then take three days for the class to rotate through the centres (Fig. 3.4).

A Three-Day Cycle

	Mon.	Tues.	Wed.	Thurs.	Fri.	Mon.
10:30-11:30	1st Rotation	3rd Rotation	5th Rotation	1st Rotation	3rd Rotation	5th Rotation
1:15-2:15	2nd Rotation	4th Rotation	6th Rotation	2nd Rotation	4th Rotation	6th Rotation

Figure 3.4

C) If your students rotate through *three* centres each day, it will take two days to complete the cycle (Fig. 3.5, page 16). With this type of schedule, your students are spending the majority of the day working at learning centres. Therefore, major areas of the curriculum must be addressed at the centres.

A Two-Day Cycle

	Mon.	**Tues.**	**Wed.**	**Thurs.**	**Fri.**
8:45-9:15	Writing	Writing	Writing	Writing	Writing
9:15-9:45	Phys. Ed.	Phys. Ed.	Phys. Ed.	Phys. Ed.	Phys. Ed.
9:45-10:15	French	French	French	French	French
10:30-11:30	1st Rotation	4th Rotation	1st Rotation	4th Rotation	1st Rotation
12:45-1:15	D.E.A.R.	D.E.A.R.	D.E.A.R.	D.E.A.R.	D.E.A.R.
1:15-2:15	2nd Rotation	5th Rotation	2nd Rotation	5th Rotation	2nd Rotation
2:30-3:30	3rd Rotation	6th Rotation	3rd Rotation	6th Rotation	3rd Rotation

Figure 3.5

EXAMPLE 2

If you monitor student movement between learning centres by a planning board or tracking sheet (refer to Chapter 7), the following timetables may prove useful.

A) Figure 3.6 outlines a separate time block for the integration of activities in language, the arts and environmental studies, as well as a separate time block for math activities.

	Mon.	**Tues.**	**Wed.**	**Thurs.**	**Fri.**
8:45-9:15	Writing	Writing	Writing	Writing	Writing
9:15-9:45	Phys. Ed.	Phys. Ed.	Phys. Ed.	Phys. Ed.	Phys. Ed.
9:45-10:15	French	French	French	French	French
10:30-11:30	**LEARNING CENTRE TIME** **(Math)**				
1:15-3:30	**LEARNING CENTRE TIME** **(Integrated Language/The Arts/Environmental Studies)**				

Figure 3.6

B) The program illustrated in Figure 3.7 indicates that students are participating in active learning situations for the greater part of the day. You must therefore ensure that all curriculum areas are addressed at the centres.

	Mon.	Tues.	Wed.	Thurs.	Fri.
8:45-9:15	Phys. Ed.	Phys. Ed.	Phys. Ed.	Phys. Ed.	Phys. Ed.
9:15-9:45	D.E.A.R.	D.E.A.R.	D.E.A.R.	D.E.A.R.	D.E.A.R.
9:45-10:15	French	French	French	French	French
10:30- 3:30	LEARNING CENTRE TIME ↕ ↕ ↕ ↕ ↕ (Integrated activities for all curriculum areas)				

Figure 3.7

4

Classroom Atmosphere

When you have created a warm, caring, and non-threatening atmosphere in your classroom, you will find that your students learn in a dynamic new way. However, creating such a desirable situation does not happen easily. There must be a gradual building of mutual respect between you and the children you teach. In part, you can achieve this by encouraging discussion, asking genuine, rather than mechanical questions, and by always looking for the best in your students. Careful planning and thought are necessary if you are to succeed.

You can help your children believe in themselves and learn to be responsible for their own actions. One way to do this is to let them participate in the establishment and ongoing monitoring of classroom rules and routines. You thereby allow them to take ownership. Children begin to realize that *all* people make mistakes and they *learn* from and through their mistakes. This encourages an atmosphere of risk taking. The onus is then on the children to take note of their own behaviour and to improve.

You can actively encourage and demonstrate the importance of co-operation by planning activities in which children *need* to co-operate. Children need to learn to co-operate, as co-operation is a life skill, a necessary and fundamental requirement in today's society.

Promoting co-operative, heterogeneous groupings in the classroom encourages children to participate in peer teaching. As children work together, they are given many opportunities to clarify their ideas. They develop better problem-solving and decision-making strategies. They gain respect for each other, are better able to appreciate another person's perspective and are more accepting of other races, genders and ethnic groups. They become more responsible, more independent and more task oriented, and they often gain a more positive attitude towards school.

Although co-operative, heterogeneous groupings are usually best for meeting the needs of your children, you will sometimes need to form homogeneous groupings. In the past, homogeneous groupings were seen to be the only way to deal with individual differences. For example, teachers grouped the good readers together, the poor readers, then all the rest. These static groups allowed teachers to program effectively, or so they thought. What they ended up with was something quite different. Their students were labelled and often carried these labels with them throughout their school years. Luckily, *flexible, temporary groupings* are now the norm rather than the exception.

Homogeneous groupings do have a place in the child-centred classroom as forums for teaching at the point of need. When you observe that some students need a particular skill or concept, you can form a *small, temporary group*. Direct teaching in this small group situation is a more effective and meaningful use of your time.

If you create a classroom that promotes respect, risk taking, peer teaching, decision making, problem solving and co-operation, you are better able to become a *facilitator of learning*. As your students experience, experiment and learn *together*, you are free to circulate, observing, analyzing, evaluating, assisting and instructing individuals and small groups.

Creating an Effective Learning Atmosphere

■ Build close relationships with your students.
- Engage them in conversations, showing that you are really interested in what they have to say.
- Ask carefully thought-out questions.
- Know when to listen and when to step in.
- Become sensitive to their needs and interests.

■ Get to know your students well by gathering information on their social, emotional, physical and cognitive abilities.
  Use the following:
- daily observation
- anecdotal records
- pre-testing
- post-testing
- work samples

■ Promote appropriate classroom behaviour by providing *genuine* praise, encouragement, and positive reinforcement whenever possible.
- CATCH SOMEONE DOING SOMETHING GOOD

NOTE: Be specific when you provide praise. Rather than making a general comment such as "I like your picture," try to point out specific areas that are noteworthy, such as "Your use of colour for your background is effective."

■ With your students brainstorm and develop rules and routines for your classroom.
  Consideration of the following list of points may prove helpful in establishing clear expectations.
- student entry into the classroom
- student tasks upon entry
  — in the morning
  — after recess
  — after lunch

- — after physical education
- — other
- student expectations
  - — in large group situations
  - — in small group activities
  - — for individual activities
  - — during indoor recess
- student activities upon task completion
- procedures for washroom exit and entry
- storage of materials
  - — students' personal belongings
  - — students' work
  - — group or class materials and resources
  - — teacher resources
- distribution of materials to students
- collection of materials
- exit and entry procedures for fire drill, gym, library
- procedures for clean-up
  - — individual/group responsibilities
  - — monitors
- student dismissal
  - — for recess
  - — for home time
  - — from the gym
  - — other
- routines and expectations for specific activities
  - — during physical education
  - — science experiments
  - — trips
  - — other

■ Encourage a team effort between the home and school to promote positive parent and student attitudes towards school and learning. (Refer to the sample letters to parents in Chapter 8.)

■ Consult educational and support personnel whenever necessary in order to obtain further information, suggestions, strategies, and program modification ideas for special needs students.
- Former teachers can provide necessary background information and strategies that have proved successful for a student in previous years.
- Special education teachers can be asked to share their expertise.
- The school nurse can provide important data, including a medical history or information regarding the home situation. The nurse can also make home visits to gather pertinent information that may have an effect on a student's progress in school.
- Psychologists can be requested to administer assessments to determine psychological, social and/or emotional strengths and difficulties.
- Principals and other available resource personnel can offer suggestions, strategies and support.
- Outside agencies can be consulted.

■ Group your students heterogeneously so that each group has students with varying abilities who are able to help and complement each other. Integrate into these groups those students with special needs (learning disabled, physically handicapped, second language learners) (Fig. 4.1).

Figure 4.1

■ Elicit from your students expectations for co-operative activities.
  Here are some tips for successful co-operative group learning:

> • We respect the rights of others in the class and in our group.
> • We never laugh at other people's mistakes.
> • We are free to make mistakes, and we learn from and through our mistakes.
> • We share resources, materials, and ideas.
> • We always help a person in the group if he/she asks for help.
> • We listen to what others have to say and ask questions if necessary.
> • We praise the efforts of others.
> • We take turns, do our share and do our best.
> • We avoid asking the teacher a question unless we have asked others in our group. (ASK THREE BEFORE ME.)

■ Plan co-operative group activities for your students and schedule them at any available horizontal or vertical block of time. (Refer to Chapter 3.)
  Here are a few co-operative group learning activities.
  NOTE: The boxes that are shaded in this book contain sample student activity cards.

EXAMPLE 1 | This social studies activity, the making of a coat of arms, is an example of an individual activity that can become a co-operative group activity. *Any* individual activity can become a co-operative group activity when your students are required to work together, and/or share their thoughts, ideas, and accomplishments with each other or with a small group (Fig. 4.2, page 22).

COAT OF ARMS
a) Draw a coat of arms.
b) Divide it into four sections.
c) In each section, draw one of the following:
 • objects associated with yourself
 • your favourite friend(s)
 • members of your family
 • things you like or identify with
d) Show your coat of arms to a partner. Have your partner guess what you have drawn. Talk about each section. Answer any questions.
e) Show your coat of arms to your group. Have others guess what you have drawn. Answer any questions.
f) Share someone else's coat of arms with another group.

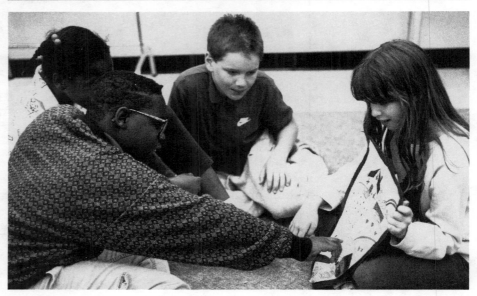

Figure 4.2

EXAMPLE 2

Any project to which the whole class can contribute becomes a co-operative group activity. Such a project might be the creation of a class mural, performance of a class play or publishing of a class newspaper. Making a class book can be a good example of a language-based, co-operative group activity (Fig. 4.3, opposite).

CLASS BOOK
a) With a partner, choose a pattern book to read. The following are suggestions:
 • *Would You Rather...*   by John Burningham
 • *Boss for a Week*   by Libby Handy
 • *The Important Book*   by Margaret Wise Brown
 • *Alligator Pie*   by Dennis Lee
b) Work together and write one page patterned after the book you have chosen.
c) Revise, edit and recopy your page.
d) Illustrate your page in a creative way.
e) Co-operate with other groups in the class to collate all completed pages into one class book.

NOTE: For other examples of pattern books, refer to the Appendix,
Favourite Children's Books.

Figure 4.3

EXAMPLE 3

Any *brainstorming* activity (whether large or small group) can encourage co-operation as the group generates ideas about a common topic.

> WHAT DO YOU KNOW ABOUT SPACE?
> In your group, record your ideas by passing a paper and pencil from one person to the next.
>
> Remember to share ideas and help other group members if they need it.

EXAMPLE 4

Students can participate in *team-building* activities, which are co-operative group activities where the prime objectives are the promotion of teamwork and co-operation. In the following three examples, students are directed to participate *without* talking and then, *with* talking. These activities serve to concretely emphasize the importance of communicating with others. At these times, you can easily address the need for appropriate noise levels in different situations (Figs. 4.4, 4.5, and 4.6, pages 24-5).

> A. SCRAMBLED SENTENCES
> a) Write one sentence about yourself on a strip of cardboard.
> b) Cut your sentence into individual word cards.
> c) Combine your cards with the rest of your group's cards.
> d) Evenly distribute the word cards to each person in your group.
> e) Try to make complete sentences using these word cards.
> NOTE Do not *talk*.
>   Do not *take* a word card from another person unless offered.
>   You can *give* word cards to others in your group.
> f) Discuss how you felt about not being able to talk. How did you help in your group?
> g) Try the activity again, but this time you may talk. Afterwards, discuss how you felt.

Figure 4.4

Figure 4.5

C. SCRAMBLED POETRY

a) Working together in your group, try to put the scrambled poem back in the right order.

NOTE Try this activity first *without* talking and then *with* talking.

b) With a partner, find another poem you like. Print each line neatly on strips of paper. Mix up the strips and put them into an envelope.

NOTE Make sure that the title, author, and name of the book that the poem is found in are printed on the envelope.
Put your names on the envelope, too, so that anyone who is having trouble can ask you for help.

Figure 4.6

EXAMPLE 5 Co-operative group learning activities can be created for *any* theme or subject area. Here is an example of a co-operative group *mathematics* activity (Fig. 4.7, page 26).

MATH — HOW FAR CAN THE CAR TRAVEL?

Materials needed
- a ball of string
- one miniature toy car
- a metre stick or measuring tape
- cards with number sentences written on them

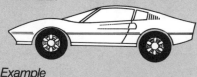

Example

5 cm + 3 cm =

Procedure

a) Decide how much time should be spent on the first round of this activity, for example, 10 minutes.

b) Place a toy car at a chosen starting point.

c) Shuffle the cards and place them in a pile on the floor near the starting point.

d) Each person takes a question card and answers it. The answer is the number of centimetres the car must be moved.

e) Using the metre stick or measuring tape, unravel the ball of string the appropriate number of centimetres. Move the car to that end point.

f) Once the time period ends, help your group members find out how far the car has travelled by measuring the total length of string used.

g) Begin again and see if you can, as a group, increase the distance the car travels.

Figure 4.7

EXAMPLE 6

The following co-operative activity, referred to as a *jigsaw* activity, involves peer teaching. Content and curriculum material in any subject area can be easily presented and mastered by students.

> ANIMAL RESEARCH
> **Part A: Group A (Home Group)**
> a) In your bin, you will find information about a particular animal. Study the material together. (Read, examine pictures, view the filmstrip, etc.)
> b) Discuss and take turns retelling interesting details learned about your animal. Become "experts" about the animal, and record some of the interesting information you have learned about it.
>
> **Part B: Jigsaw**
> a) Number each person in your group 1 to 5. Remember your number.
> b) Meet with classmates who have the same number you do.
> c) Present your original group's information to this new group.
> d) Listen to the members of this group as one by one they tell you about their animals.

■ After any co-operative group activity, have the students *evaluate* their individual contributions to the group as well as their success in the total group process. Figures 4.8 and 4.9 are examples of written evaluation forms that might be used by students:

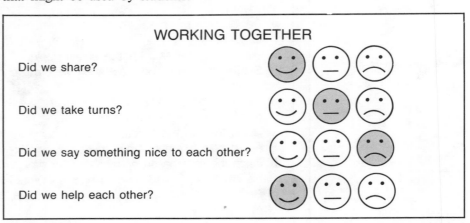

WORKING TOGETHER

Did we share?

Did we take turns?

Did we say something nice to each other?

Did we help each other?

Figure 4.8

Name __Jennifer__

Date __Mar. 9__

Group Members' Names __Nadia__
__Edson__
__Steven__

1. I listened to others while they were speaking.   ☑

2. I offered my own ideas and information.   ☑

3. I asked others for their ideas.   ☑

4. I shared the materials and supplies.   ☑

5. I asked my group for help when I needed it.   ☐

6. I helped someone in my group.   ☑

7. I took my turn and encouraged others to take their turns.   ☑

8. I praised someone in the group.   ☐

Figure 4.9

■ Form small homogeneous groupings of students when necessary, in order to teach specific skills at a particular time. Remember that these groupings should be flexible and temporary.

Here are a few examples.

EXAMPLE 1   You can pull together into a small, temporary group those students who are using speech regularly in their writing but are not using quotation marks. Demonstrate the proper use of quotation marks using the students' own writing as examples.

EXAMPLE 2   You can pull together into a small, temporary group those students experiencing difficulty in understanding the concept of multiplication. In this way, you can provide more individualized, varied instruction based on needs.

Whole Language

In a child-centred classroom, children can see and understand the interrelationships between reading, writing, listening, speaking, viewing, and dramatizing. They acquire language, both oral and written, from the whole to the parts, by dealing with relevant experiences, issues, and reading material. They are able to integrate their skills into all content areas of the curriculum. As a result, their learning becomes more meaningful.

In these surroundings and situations, children read with fluency and for enjoyment. They understand the importance of and need for reading in today's society. They write with clarity, imagination, and in an organized manner. They *want* to write because they have a purpose and an audience for their writing. Once they become authors, writing becomes a motivational tool for development in all other areas of language.

With an *equal emphasis* placed on listening and speaking, children learn to talk with confidence. They are able to organize their thoughts and convey information in both formal and informal situations. They become active listeners and reflective speakers by listening attentively and selectively, thinking critically, and responding to the ideas of others.

Whole language has a profound effect on all aspects of the curriculum, and as you implement this philosophy, you will see your children becoming more motivated and excited in every aspect of the school program.

i) Creating a Language-rich Environment

■ Ensure that your classroom environment is rich in print and language-stimulating possibilities. (For examples of excellent print and language-stimulating resources, see the Appendix, Favourite Children's Books.)

Try to offer a wide variety of the following materials and resources (Fig. 5.1, opposite).

- fiction books
- novel sets
- poetry
- picture books
- big books
- wordless books
- predictable books
- pattern books
- anthologies
- books with accompanying tapes or records

- non-fiction books
- student-written materials
- recipe books
- encyclopedias
- dictionaries
- thesauri
- magazines
- newspapers
- telephone directories
- television guides
- catalogues
- signs
- labels
- posters
- lists
- challenge cards
- message boards
- felt boards
- magnetic boards
- mailboxes
- writing centre (paper, writing tools, ideas for writing)
- student author display
- library corner
- puppets
- drama/dress-up area
- audio-visual equipment

Figure 5.1

ii) Creating Reflective Speaking Experiences

■ Provide frequent opportunities for *oral language* development by allowing students to express, clarify and rehearse their thoughts and ideas verbally.

They can participate in reflective speaking in the following settings or circumstances:

- large and small group discussions
- problem-solving activities
- activities with blocks, puzzles, games, toys
- sand and water activities
- a talking centre
- a puppet centre
- a dress-up centre/drama centre
- a construction centre
- a nature centre
- felt or magnetic board activities (Fig. 5.2)
- the use of individual cassette tapes for each student to record oral language samples

Figure 5.2

iii) Creating Active Listening Experiences

■ Provide opportunities for *active listening* experiences. As students listen and reflect, encourage them to respond by thinking, talking, and doing.

Offer a variety of the following experiences:

• listening with headphones to tape-recorders or record players (Fig. 5.3)
• frequent opportunities to experience literature in read-aloud situations
• echo clapping activities
• following oral directions
• viewing filmstrips
• questioning and conferencing sessions
• storytelling activities
• felt or magnetic board activities
• role-playing and dramatizing experiences

Figure 5.3

iv) Creating Focussed Viewing Experiences

■ Provide opportunities for *focussed viewing,* and allow time for reflection and sharing.

Here is a range of focussed viewing possibilities:

- books (illustrations, format, organization)
- pictures
- photos
- slides
- filmstrips (Fig. 5.4)
- films
- videos
- TV programs/commercials
- plays/theatre
- outdoor excursions (using cameras, binoculars)
- science experiments (using magnifying glasses, microscopes, telescopes) (Fig. 5.5)

Figure 5.4

Figure 5.5

v) Creating Reflective Dramatizing Experiences

■ Provide opportunities for *drama and related creative activities*.
   You can introduce any of the following:

- role playing
- movement
- dress-up centre (Fig. 5.6)
- puppet centre (Fig. 5.7)
- storytelling
- tableau (creating a situation or scene and freezing)
- drama centre
- dance
- music
- mime

Figure 5.6

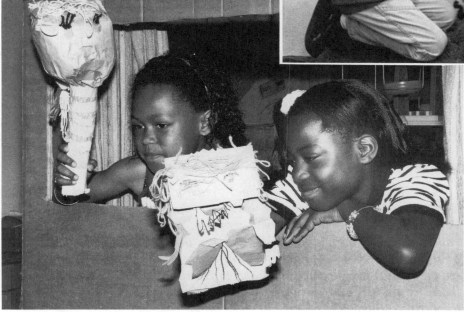

Figure 5.7

vi) Creating Meaningful Reading Experiences

■ Ensure that your reading corner is well stocked with a wide variety of children's literature. You might want to include some of the titles listed in the Appendix of this book.

For other more complete listings of literature, refer to:

The Read-Aloud Handbook, Jim Trelease (Penguin, 1983)
Growing with Books (Ontario Ministry of Education, 1988)
Children's Literature in the Elementary School, Fourth Edition, Charlotte S. Huck (Holt, Rinehart & Winston, 1987)
Michele Landsberg's Guide to Children's Books, Michele Landsberg (Penguin Books, 1986)
Too Good To Miss: Classic Canadian Children's Books (The Canadian Children's Book Centre, Toronto)
Our Choice/Your Choice (The Canadian Children's Book Centre, Toronto)

■ Make available a variety of *non-fiction* reading materials at varying levels of difficulty to correspond to themes or curriculum units of study.

■ Devote a section of your reading corner to *student-authored* books. (Fig. 5.8)

Figure 5.8

NOTE: When your students write and "publish" their own books, they can see the link between reading and writing. Students, as authors, reinforce skills they need in order to become proficient readers. They bring a new understanding to their own reading, because they have first-hand knowledge of and experience with the development of story lines, characterization, and setting, as well as with prediction and inference. Students often become more comfortable and motivated when reading and rereading their own and their peers' writing.

■ Provide for a wide variety of *daily reading experiences* such as:

Read-aloud   (Fig. 5.9)
Daily read-aloud experiences (occurring several times each day) expose students to literature and models of good reading behaviours (intonation of voice, expression, fluency, enjoyment, etc.)

Figure 5.9

Group Reading   (Fig. 5.10)
Students can participate in whole class or small group oral reading of big books, stories, poems, songs, language experience chart stories, etc. As students read together, they are not singled out, but begin to feel more confident in the group.

NOTE: Avoid "round-robin" reading sessions. Having students read orally, one at a time, in a group is not *conducive to creating a positive attitude towards reading. Students can experience anxiety and frustration when they are reading orally without having time to rehearse. Group reading provides the necessary rehearsal time to build confidence.*

Figure 5.10

Singing and Chanting   (Fig. 5.11)

As students sing, read and/or chant together, they become more aware of the rhythm and pattern of language. Words to songs and poems can be put onto paper and stored in booklets for students to read and reread. Songs and poems can either be cut into strips or each line or word copied onto cards; they can then be stored in envelopes to be put back into the right order. (Refer to the "Scrambled Poetry" activity in Chapter 4.)

NOTE: Good resources to use for group reading and for singing and chanting are Chime In *by Jean Malloch (Doubleday Canada, 1981) and* Books Alive *by Jean and Ian Malloch (Doubleday Canada, 1986).*

Figure 5.11

Paired Reading   (Fig. 5.12)

The experience of reading together in pairs allows students opportunities to read and discuss in a risk-free atmosphere. The more fluent readers will often take leadership roles while the beginning and developing readers gain valuable exposure to higher levels of reading material. Paired reading is an ideal way to promote the reading of novels or "chapter books."

Figure 5.12

Predictable and Pattern Book Reading (Fig. 5.13)

Students begin to see the patterns in language as they hear, read and internalize the patterns in predictable books and pattern books. These reading experiences can lead to meaningful talking and writing extensions. (Refer to "Class Book" in Chapter 4.)

Figure 5.13

D.E.A.R.* Drop Everything and Read (Fig. 5.14 a and b)

Giving students time for pleasure reading helps establish and nurture a love of reading. Students should be provided with daily opportunities to select and peruse books at their leisure.

* This term was introduced by Andrea Butler and Jan Turbill in *Towards a Reading-Writing Classroom* (Australia: Primary English Teaching Association, 1984), p. 49.

Figure 5.14(a)

Figure 5.14(b)

■ Allow time for flexible conferences where you and groups of students share, discuss and celebrate what they are reading (Fig. 5.15).

Figure 5.15

Reading Records and Reading Responses

■ Provide students with reading record sheets or reading response logs or journals to record their reactions to what they have read (Fig. 5.16 and Fig. 5.17).

EXAMPLE 1

READING RECORD			Name _Sandi_
Date	Pages Read	Title	Comments
Mar. 9	15	Banner in the Sky	So far, what a great beginning I like Rudi. He reminds me of my friend Joe.

Figure 5.16

EXAMPLE 2

> Mar. 3 1989
> I just finished reading Sadako and the Thousand Cranes. It was great but I dont understand why she had to die.
>
> Did you realize that this is a true story? How did you feel when you found out she was dying?
> M.B.

Figure 5.17 Reading Response Log

NOTE: In reading response logs, students write the thoughts, feelings, questions and insights that they have had in response to their reading. The teacher can respond in writing and by so doing invites the student to write further (Fig. 5.18).

Figure 5.18

Open-ended Reading Activities

■ Provide open-ended activities that promote the skills of comprehending, predicting, inferring, hypothesizing, and drawing conclusions. Each activity should be discussed with the students (and in some cases modelled or demonstrated) before it is offered as a possible choice.

NOTE: Since you want to encourage students to read for enjoyment, you should not feel that every reading experience must be followed by a written activity.

Here are some sample open-ended reading activities:

Pretend you are having a telephone conversation with a friend. Tell her/him about the story you have just read. Tape your conversation at the listening centre.

Read the first chapter or first few pages of a story. Predict what will happen next. Record your prediction by writing or taping. Read on and check to see if you were right.

Do you feel that this story has an effective ending? Why or why not? Have a debate with someone who thinks differently than you.

Draw at least 3 pictures that illustrate the story line of your book. Shuffle them and have a partner put them in the right sequence. Store the pictures in an envelope.

With a partner, practise *telling* the story to an audience. Schedule a time for sharing.

How would you feel if you were one of the characters in the story? As that character, answer questions posed by others who have read or heard the story.

Design a poster recommending your book to others.

Write a letter to your pen pal telling about the story you have just read.

Create a diorama illustrating a scene from your book (Fig. 5.19).

Figure 5.19

■ Schedule time for writing daily. Setting a specific block of time and planning frequent writing experiences at other times of the day and in all areas of the curriculum will help ensure that writing becomes ongoing and valued (Fig. 5.20).

Figure 5.20

NOTE: Very *young writers should not be expected to write at the same time. Writing opportunities should be provided throughout the day. By placing a message pad near a toy phone in the house centre or by leaving stationery near a mailbox, you can encourage even the youngest student to write.*

■ With your students, discuss writing as a process and suggest that they will be going through some of the same phases of writing as professional authors—pre-writing, drafting, revising, editing, and publishing for an audience.

a) Pre-writing
Students search for, contemplate, and choose topics to write about. They experience, discuss, brainstorm, question, rehearse, and clarify their ideas. They engage in a variety of storytelling and role-playing activities.

b) Drafting
This phase is the write-it-down-as-fast-as-you-can phase. Here, the emphasis is clearly on the *content* and meaning.

c) Revising

During this phase, students are encouraged to "revisit," or take another look at, the *content* of their writing. They can then change, add to, and improve their initial drafts.

d) Editing

When students, in collaboration with the teacher, decide to present and share their writing with an audience, they recognize the need to edit—to proofread and polish the *mechanics* of their writing.

e) Publishing and Sharing

Students present their chosen pieces of writing to an audience.

NOTE: Not every piece of writing will go through all phases of the process. Beginning writers might only participate in the pre-writing, drafting and sharing phases. Also, some writing is not meant to be shared, such as personal writing and reflections. You need to be aware of each writer's developmental stages and to help him or her understand the purpose or intention of the writing.

Fostering Daily Writing

- Allow students to choose their own topics for writing by providing:
  - stimulating objects, pictures, photos, films, filmstrips, books, magazines, newspapers, etc.
  - storytelling experiences
  - opportunities for role playing
  - opportunities for picture making and creative art to generate discussion and idea flow
  - meaningful experiences such as class events, trips, group activities, performances, etc.
  - opportunities for brainstorming in a variety of situations

- Become a writer yourself and thus serve as a model for your students.
  - Make lists with your students.
  - Write messages or letters to your students and parents. (Use school or personalized stationery, or use Post-its for brief comments and questions about students' work.)
  - Do your own personal writing (poems, stories, jokes, etc.), and share.

- Become a storyteller for your students and *model* storytelling skills. Encourage children to become effective storytellers.

  NOTE: A good resource to use to improve storytelling techniques is Tell Me Another *by Bob Barton (Pembroke Publishers, 1986).*

- Provide your students with writing folders, either commercially produced or student made, to serve as working files throughout the process. An effectively designed folder has two or three pockets which may contain and organize draft writing, edited and polished pieces, topic ideas or lists, ongoing records, titles of books, and/or lists of most commonly used words (Fig. 5.21, opposite).

Figure 5.21

■ In one area of the classroom, set up a wide variety of writing materials.
Here are some materials you might want to include:

- paper—in a variety of colours, sizes and shapes; blank and lined, ready-made booklets
- writing tools—pencils, pens, markers, chalk, etc.
- writing ideas—class-generated ideas listed on posters or charts, an idea table with real objects to stimulate discussion, theme books and materials, etc.
- publishing materials—stapler, cardboard, mactac, wallpaper, string, wool, dental floss and needles (to sew books together), art supplies

■ Through modelling, discussion and experimentation, develop with your students strategies for draft writing.
Here are some helpful ideas:

- Suggest that students write down their thoughts and ideas as quickly as they can.
- Suggest that they *cross out* any words, phrases, sentences or paragraphs that need changing.
- Encourage them not to use an eraser, which would slow down idea flow.
- Suggest that they write on every other line to allow space for revision.
- Have young children write on blank paper and older students use the lined paper that they are comfortable with.
- Use loose-leaf paper (rather than a notebook) and only one side of the paper to facilitate revising, cutting, pasting, and reorganization of writing.

■ Encourage and accept all attempts at writing based on the developmental stages of your students (Fig. 5.22).

Scribble Stage	*cell u n ~*
Random Letter Stage	X P + D Z D
Consonants Stage	+ b w d t s
Phonetic Spelling Stage	the bo wt dn the stt
Conventional Spelling Stage	the boy went don the street.

Figure 5.22   Stages of Spelling

NOTE: The use of scribble and/or approximate spelling allows even very young children to believe that they are writers. When children are encouraged to try to spell the words they need, they are encouraged to experiment with sounds and words. They become risk takers, drawing upon all the knowledge and literary experiences they have already had.

■ Encourage students to write down all the sounds that they hear. If they are reluctant to use approximate spelling, encourage them to write the initial consonant and draw a line for the rest of the word (Fig. 5.23). They can later go back and fill in the remaining letters.

Figure 5.23

■ Encourage peer and group interaction by establishing with the students routines and expectations for writing conferences.

EXAMPLE 1   Invite the students to choose partners and sit down somewhere in the room. Have them tell their stories to their partners and answer any questions they may be asked.

EXAMPLE 2   If students need someone to talk with about their writing-in-progress, encourage them to ask a class member to meet with them at a talking area (on the carpet or at a table) where they won't disturb others who are working quietly (Fig. 5.24).

Figure 5.24

■ Make flexible writing conferences an integral part of your language time block. You and small groups of students can discuss, share, revise, edit, and/or celebrate writing at these meetings (Fig. 5.25).

Figure 5.25

■ Teach strategies for revising story lines by modelling good questioning techniques. Encourage students to ask who, what, when, where, why and how questions during writing conferences. Introduce and encourage the use of model questions such as "And then what happened?" and "How did you feel at the end of the story?"

NOTE: Good opportunities for modelling occur during the reading of good literature to the class, and during any conferences or discussions with individuals and/or groups.

■ Teach "mini-lessons"* to *large groups*, *small groups* or *individual* students. You may want to discuss particular needs that you notice in their writing and to expose them to specific concepts, skills, or strategies involving issues arising in both content and mechanics throughout all phases of writing.

* Lucy McCormick Calkins introduces and illustrates mini-lessons in her book *The Art of Teaching Writing* (Heinemann Educational Books, Portsmouth, New Hampshire, 1986).

The following are possible mini-lesson demonstrations.

Content
- questioning techniques to help extend story lines
- sequencing of story lines
- the use of descriptive vocabulary
- the use of flashbacks

Mechanics
- spelling strategies
- the use of quotation marks for dialogue
- how to avoid run-on sentences

Publishing
- division of a story into pages to prepare for publication
- text illustrations
- publishing formats

NOTE: Skill-building mini-lessons during the editing *phase should not be confused with traditional grammar lessons which were customarily followed by textbook or fill-in-the-blank worksheet assignments. These busy-work types of exercises produced little transfer of learning into daily work. However, in the mini-lesson approach, students are introduced to a particular skill at a time when they are using and/or need to learn the skill. Those who are ready are encouraged to apply it in their* own *writing.*

■ Allow students to frequently present their writing in some polished or published format.

Publishing possibilities open to them might include:

- posters
- letters
- plays
- commercials
- advertisements
- banners
- charts
- home-made filmstrips (Students record their writing and illustrations on acetate pages taped together. They use an overhead projector to project their stories onto the screen.)
- books (Students may choose from among hard-cover books, soft-cover books, picture books, big books, co-operative class books, and pattern books.)

- movie box (Students make a box to represent a television, then record their stories on paper and tape the papers together in lengths. When each end of a story is attached to a long paper roll or stick, the story can be moved along by turning one of the sticks.)

■ Introduce a planning board to help focus and organize students as they move through the various phases of writing (Fig. 5.26).

When students finish a phase, they move their name cards to the appropriate pocket on the planning board. Upon completion of one piece of writing, they begin another. They decide whether or not to publish and share. They write one piece of writing after another and begin to understand that writing is a continuous, ongoing process.

NOTE: The arrows on the planning board indicate that this is not a linear process. Rather, students flow back and forth among all the phases of the process.

Figure 5.26

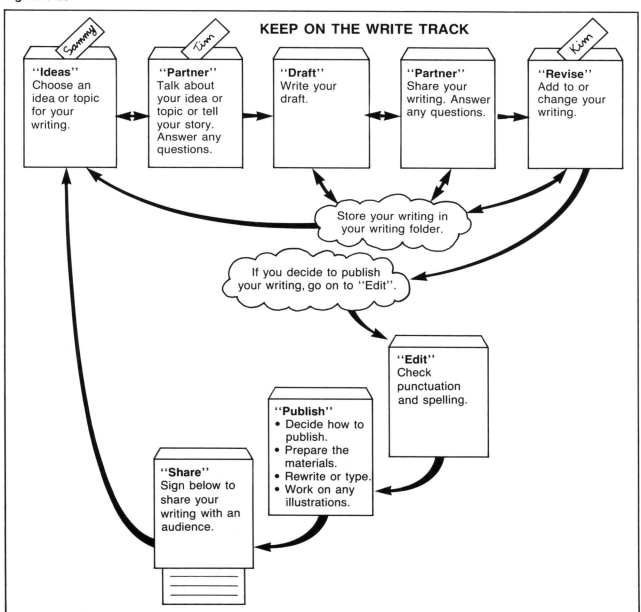

KEEP ON THE WRITE TRACK

Sammy

"Ideas" Choose an idea or topic for your writing.

Tim

"Partner" Talk about your idea or topic or tell your story. Answer any questions.

"Draft" Write your draft.

"Partner" Share your writing. Answer any questions.

Kim

"Revise" Add to or change your writing.

Store your writing in your writing folder.

If you decide to publish your writing, go on to "Edit".

"Edit" Check punctuation and spelling.

"Publish"
- Decide how to publish.
- Prepare the materials.
- Rewrite or type.
- Work on any illustrations.

"Share" Sign below to share your writing with an audience.

■ Ensure that all writing is purposeful and relevant to the child's experiences. Keeping this in mind, try to introduce your students to all modes of writing. Key modes are as follows:

- Expressive writing, which is speech-like and subjective, conveys personal thoughts, ideas, and feelings. Journal writing, personal letters and logs are examples.
- Transactional writing, which is impersonal and objective, explains, informs, or persuades. Lists, reports, instructions, business letters, and recipes are examples.
- Poetic writing, in which style and form are important, includes forms of literature such as poetry, short stories, novels, scripts and biographies.

■ *Integrate* language into all curriculum areas by ensuring that reading, writing, listening, speaking, viewing, and dramatizing are included in all areas of your program. (Refer to Chapter 6.)

6

An Integrated Child-centred Curriculum

T he key to planning an integrated child-centred curriculum is *balance*—a balance among large group, small group and individual activities, a balance in curriculum and content areas, and a balance between teacher-directed and child-initiated experiences.

Although a great portion of this book pertains to small group and individual work, this does not mean that you should overlook the value of whole class (large group) experiences. All three kinds of experiences help children function and learn in any real-life situation.

When considering your long-range plans, you should ensure that each of the main curriculum areas—Environmental Studies, Communications and the Arts—receives equal attention. Each of these *main* curriculum areas also contains specific *content* areas which need to be balanced. In your Environmental Studies curriculum, for example, social studies and science require equal emphasis over the course of the year.

Although each curriculum area contains specific content and skills that children need to learn, the *process* of learning that occurs in *all* curriculum areas is the same. That is to say, in all curriculum areas, children experience, communicate, interact, reflect, observe, explore, follow directions, predict, solve problems, make decisions, etc. This list is endless! Therefore, integrating various curriculum areas will help you achieve the balance so necessary for effective programming.

Once you take the time to ensure that you have a balanced program, you will probably want to examine curriculum documents, teacher resources and available student materials. By doing this, you will become more knowledgeable about your board's policies and about the resources available to you. By collecting and preparing materials needed beforehand, you will be more organized and ready to meet your students' daily needs.

The balance between teacher-directed and child-initiated learning is of utmost importance in creating an integrated, child-centred curriculum. One of the primary goals of a child-centred approach is to encourage children to develop greater decision-making and problem-solving skills, thus promoting greater independence. However, you should not abdicate your responsibilities to guide, to sometimes initiate and to always respond to the needs of your students.

Before beginning an integrated, child-centred unit, you might want to ask your students what they already know, what they need or want to know, and how they think their needs might be met. You are, in essence, negotiating the curriculum with your students, and throughout the program, your students should be encouraged to assess, evaluate, shape, reshape and restructure their own learning opportunites.

When the planning of an integrated, child-centred curriculum is done *with* the children and *by* the children, the curriculum, the themes, the activities and the active learning experiences become more relevant, because they are built on the backgrounds, interests and everyday life experiences of each individual student. Children move towards the goal of becoming life-long learners as they gain a positive attitude towards school.

By using a multitude of methods to expand your integrated, child-centred curriculum, you will become better able to see where the interests of your students lie, the subject areas that will be covered, and the active learning types of experiences possible. You will become better able to maintain the *balance* necessary, and you will become a partner and guide in the learning process, learning along with your students.

Creating an Integrated Child-centred Curriculum

Choosing a Theme or Topic

■ Choose a theme or topic to explore by examining your board's curriculum requirements, brainstorming with your students for possible areas that they would like to explore, or using the "spontaneity of the moment"—for example, when a child brings a butterfly into the classroom, you can initiate a science unit on insects.

■ Examine the available teacher resources, curriculum documents and student materials related to the topic.

■ Brainstorm (with teaching partners, if available) for words associated with the chosen topic. Organize the ideas in the form of a web (Fig. 6.1, opposite top).

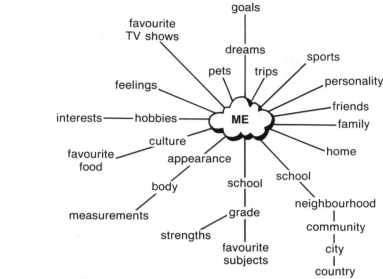

Figure 6.1 Word Association Web

Ensuring Active Learning

■ In order to visualize various active learning experiences for your unit, list active, "doing" words, such as *investigating, exploring, demonstrating, celebrating, designing, creating, observing* and *constructing**.

These words, are found in the document *Ages 9 Through 12*, prepared by the Ontario Public School Teachers' Federation and the Ontario Ministry of Education, 1986.

■ Brainstorm (with teaching partners, if available) for specific activities pertaining to your topic under the different action words listed. Organize your ideas in the form of a web (Fig. 6.2).

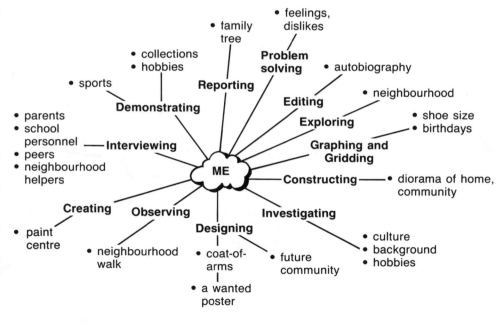

Figure 6.2 Active Learning Web

■ Using different colours, identify the subject areas that you have included in your active learning web. For example, circle all language activities in red and all social studies activities in blue (Fig. 6.3).

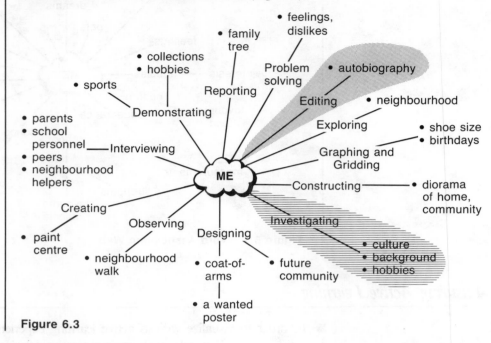

Figure 6.3

■ If you need to clarify the colour-coded web, organize the activities in the form of a subject area web (Fig. 6.4).

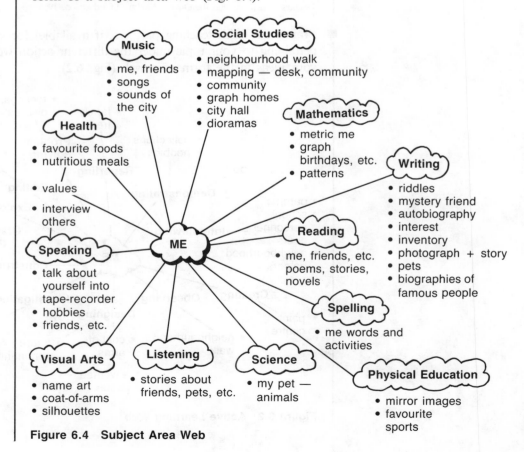

Figure 6.4 Subject Area Web

■ Using a Venn diagram, identify activities from the webs as large group, small group and/or individual. The Venn diagram facilitates planning and provides a graphic reminder of the balance and variety necessary in effective programming (Fig. 6.5).

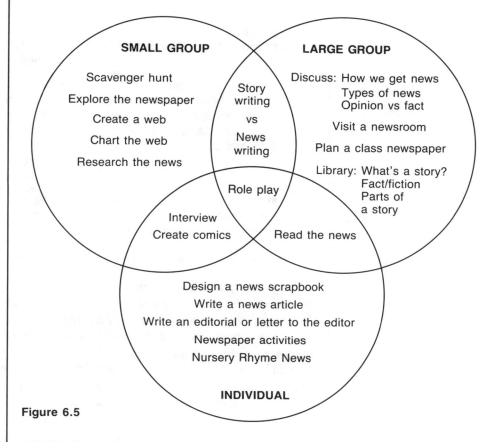

Figure 6.5

NOTE: Some activities will overlap in the sense that they can span more than one type of student grouping. For example, an activity might begin as a large group learning experience, but extend into a small group and/or individual activity. Also, students may be given a choice of working at a certain activity individually or with a group. The overlapping sections of the Venn diagram allow you to concretely represent the possibilities.

Planning Your Integrated Curriculum

■ Brainstorm with your students to find out what they already know about the topic and what they would like to know, and modify your activities accordingly.

■ With the students' assistance, collect, sort, and prepare the resources and materials needed for the unit.

■ Order any movies that would be relevant to the theme, making sure they are appropriate to your students' maturity level and interests.

■ Book any out-of-classroom excursions that would extend your students' learning about the topic.

■ Prepare a flexible plan, sequencing the activities selected for your unit. Keep in mind the learning objectives of each activity.

EXAMPLE 1

Activities	Objectives
1 At a building centre have children explore with small blocks. Observe.	• to find out what the children already know about buildings, communities, etc.
2 With the large group, go on a neighbourhood walk and have children carefully observe and collect data as to what makes up their own community.	• to promote critical observation • to demonstrate and reinforce the recording of data • to extend knowledge of the concept of community • to promote greater awareness of the environment
3 In pairs or small groups, have children analyze the data collected on their walk and graph the results.	• to develop skills of graphing and analysis

NOTE: This planning procedure represents one *method of planning a unit. In no way should it be construed as a set day plan to be followed in a lock-step fashion. Planning a child-centred integrated unit requires that you take into account the past experiences, needs, interests, learning styles and expectations of your particular group of students. Some students may take one day to accomplish a certain activity; others may take a week. Also, once you are well into the unit, you may find that the order of activities must be changed. Flexibility is important.*

■ You may want to use a long-range planning sheet such as Figure 6.6 (opposite) to ensure a balance of curriculum and content areas.

NOTE: This planning sheet is effective in illustrating the balance *necessary in curriculum and content areas over the course of the year. When using this planning sheet, you will need to keep in mind the many possibilities for integration.*

Curriculum Areas	Content Areas		Fall	Winter	Summer
Communications	Mathematics	Number	Adding, Sub., counting, estimation, place value		
		Measurement	Linear –measure "me" – desk, class – our wt. Kg. mass graphing		
		Geometry	Flat Shape solid shape structures pattern blocks geoboards		
	Language — Listening, Speaking, Reading, Writing, Viewing, Dramatizing		–reading friendship books "me" poems student – pubs. – writing personal stories, journals responses – storytelling – focus on books, authors, print, publishing		
The Arts	Dramatic Arts		role playing "Round Trip" mime mirror group dynamics		
	Visual Arts		name art silhouettes paperplate people line design symmetry modelling colour		
	Music		Songs "You are My Friend" "Climb Every Mt." rhythm instrument lummi sticks (chants)		
	Physical Education/Health Education		movement small equipment soccer skills favourite foods nutrition – balanced diet		
Environmental Studies	Science		Structures expt – towers, bridges using different materials straw plastic pins wood sticks plastic stirs		
	Social Studies		Me family neighborhood community mapping skills – desk, class, school, community interviewing skills community helpers		

Figure 6.6

7

Learning Centres

Effective learning centres allow children opportunities to interact, share, and co-operate with each other. Students become involved in peer teaching and gain valuable leadership skills. There is little pressure to compete with others because this approach to learning emphasizes co-operation. The goal is for children to do their best for *their* own benefit and for the benefit of the group.

Your students will gain a greater willingness to take risks in these small group situations. As they gain confidence in their own abilities, they will become more self-motivated and independent and will begin to evaluate themselves more critically. When presented with a *choice* of learning activities at various levels of difficulty, they will begin to take greater responsibility for their own learning, becoming better decision makers and problem solvers.

As the tasks become more active, the experiences can become more meaningful and relevant to your students' cognitive stages of development. They are encouraged to use every facet of communication. They experiment, experience, question, discuss and reflect, thus participating in the process of discovery learning, the process of "learning how to learn."

Collecting learning materials is much easier with a centred approach because resources are shared to a much greater extent and only a few students need the same materials at any one time. It is no longer necessary to purchase *class* sets of workbooks and reading programs which rarely meet students' individual needs and interests. Instead, funds can be used to acquire class libraries of literature; science equipment such as magnifying glasses; thermometers; measuring instruments; manipulative math materials; magnetic boards; and other items.

As your learning centres become an increasingly integral part of your overall program, you will become accustomed to a variety of activities occurring at the same time in different areas of the room. As you become more comfortable with this approach, you can circulate, encourage, instruct small groups and individuals, and promote independence. Your role will begin to change from that of imparter of knowledge to *facilitator* of learning and you will become a full partner in the learning process.

Creating Effective Learning Centres

■ Examine your timetable and choose *one* vertical time block to introduce students to a small group, learning centred approach.

■ Allow for *input sessions* prior to learning centre time. During these input sessions, centre tasks are introduced, specific skills are taught, or large group theme-related activities occur. When introducing new activities at various centres, stagger the instructional input over a few days. By doing so, your input sessions will not become overly long and unwieldly.

■ Allow time for *sharing* after each learning centre time.

■ Beginning with the integrated child-centred curriculum that you have planned (refer to Chapter 6), select large group, small group and individual activities appropriate for the individual needs and interests of your students.

■ Decide on the number of learning centres or small group activities that you want to set up in the classroom.

■ Decide on the maximum number of students allowed at each centre at any one time.

NOTE: An ideal number of students at each centre is four, five or six. (Refer to Chapter 4.)

■ Decide on the name and content of each centre.

NOTE: When centres are first introduced to a class or are first used by a teacher not accustomed to this approach, it is recommended that centre activities require a minimum of teacher direction. Students beginning to work in centres need to learn routines, expectations and responsibilities, need to strengthen self-direction and independence, and need to develop good attitudes towards learning and working at centres.

The following boxes identify several kinds of centres and materials each might contain.

Reading Centre
- wide variety of reading material (refer to Chapter 5)
- student-authored books
- reading logs to record books read
- tape-recorders and individual cassette tapes to record read-aloud selections by students

---

Writing/Publishing Centre
- a variety of materials to write on and to write with
- date stamp
- draft stamp
- word lists
- thesauri, dictionaries
- publishing materials
- mailbox and stationery

Math Centre (Figure 7.1)
- manipulative math materials such as pattern blocks, tangrams, blocks, junk materials, etc.
- recording sheets
- graph paper
- measuring tools
- geometric shapes
- two-dimensional and three-dimensional materials
- variety of math text books

Figure 7.1

Puppetry Centre
- puppet theatre
- variety of puppets (teacher-made, student-made, and commercially produced)
- puppet-making materials such as cardboard, sticks, paper bags, odd socks, bits of fabric, etc.

Art Centre
- multi-media materials
- a wide variety of art tools and paper
- two-dimensional and three-dimensional materials such as boxes, scraps, fabric, etc.

Nature Centre
- large magnifying glasses
- outdoor-found materials
- recording sheets for observations

Many kinds of centres can be created. Here are a few other possibilities:

Invention Centre

Science Centre (Figure 7.2)

Magnets Centre

Structure Centre

Sand Centre (Figure 7.3)

Figure 7.2

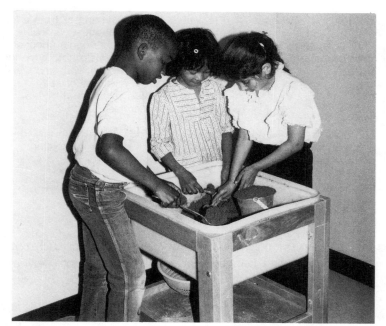

Figure 7.3

Water Centre

Blocks Centre

Drama/Dress-up Centre

Mapping Centre

Take-apart Centre

NOTE: Some centres may be permanent *such as the listening centre, reading corner, and art area; some may be* portable, *perhaps stored in bins, buckets, or on a table and easily moved; and some may be* temporary, *used for a specific purpose for a short period of time.*

■ Examine the tasks and activities at the centres carefully to ensure that they are child-centred, represent active learning, provide opportunities for student choice, include open-ended tasks (no right answers) and provide opportunities for manipulation of concrete materials.

Figure 7.4 illustrates the differences between teacher-directed and child-centred tasks.

Centre Name	Teacher-directed Tasks	Child-centred Tasks
Reading	The teacher selects the stories for the students to read and assigns follow-up tasks.	Students choose their own reading materials from a wide variety of resources. They fill in their reading record sheets or reading response logs. They may then devise appropriate follow-up work from a list of tasks generated by the students and teacher.
Writing	The teacher assigns a topic for story-writing.	Students draw upon their personal and classroom experiences and interests to determine their own writing topics.
Math	The teacher assigns a math worksheet to be completed.	Students select from a variety of concrete materials and create their own patterns.
Spelling	The teacher assigns a word list and students write their words in alphabetical order.	From their personal writing or from a list of words generated about a particular theme being studied, students choose several words that they do not know how to spell. They experiment with and work with the words in a variety of self-selected activities established by the students and teacher.
Art	Children are shown how to make bear puppets using paper bags and construction paper.	A wide variety of materials are provided. Children make their own interesting inventions.

Figure 7.4

■ Collect, sort and prepare the materials and resources needed for each centre. Once you are comfortable with learning centres in your classroom, involve the students in the acquisition and preparation of materials. The following charts may help with organization.

EXAMPLE 1

THINGS TO DO FOR THE ___*Structures*___ CENTRE

Materials to Collect		Things to Prepare

Equipment

- [✓] paper
- [✓] pencils
- [✓] crayons
- [✓] scissors
- [✓] glue
- [✓] filmstrip projector
- [ ]

Manipulative Materials

- [✓] straws
- [✓] pipe cleaners
- [✓] pins
- [✓] Plasticene
- [✓] junk (boxes, tubes)
- [✓] wooden stir sticks
- [✓] plastic stir sticks
- [ ]

Things to Prepare

- [✓] signs
- [✓] task cards
- [✓] student work-sheets
- [✓] games
- [✓] student folders/scrapbook
- [ ]
- [ ]
- [ ]

Student Resources

- [✓] Books on Structures
- [✓] Filmstrip "Structures in Toronto"
- [✓] Picture File "City Structures"
- [ ]
- [ ]
- [ ]

Figure 7.5

EXAMPLE 2

Name of Centre	Activities at Centre	Materials Needed
Structures	*Build a structure as tall as you can (towers, bridges)*	*Straws* *Pipe cleaners*

Figure 7.6

■ Decide *where* the centres would best be located and prepare for use.

NOTE: Centres do not need to be set up in specific areas of the classroom. If space is limited, all materials necessary for the centres can be stored in bins, buckets, folders, or other portable containers and located in one central area. These containers can then be taken by the students to any area in the room or to a designated work space. Matching the labels on the containers to the work spaces in the room aids organization and management. The library can also be used as a designated area for small group/centre work.

■ For each centre, decide with the students where to *store* and *display* their work. (Refer to Chapter 2.)

■ Decide how best to begin moving your students through centres. The following examples provide a variety of methods to help both the students and the teacher become accustomed to the routines associated with students moving *to* and *through* centres.

NOTE: There is no one *method of initiating and operating a learning-centred approach in your classroom.*

EXAMPLE 1

ROTATION SYSTEM
A rotation system, whereby all students systematically move through centres, allows teachers greater control over *when* and *where* students will work. A group rotation method ensures participation by *all* students in *all* centres over a specified period of time. It also allows the teacher and the students to become accustomed to many things occurring simultaneously in the room.

a) Write group names on cards and post on a chart or board using tape, pins or magnets (Fig. 7.7). (Magnets may be taped to the back of cards for easy movement on a magnetic blackboard.) Prepare centre name cards and attach them to the board or chart. As the groups rotate through the centres, move all the name cards forward so that the chart reflects the rotation cycle.

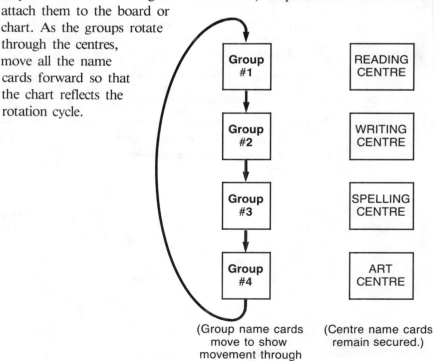

(Group name cards move to show movement through centres.)

(Centre name cards remain secured.)

Figure 7.7

b) The inner circle of this *rotation wheel* contains group names. The outer circle contains centre names which can be written on cards attached to the wheel by paper clips or clothespins to allow for frequent changes. The two circles are attached in the centre by a paper fastener (Fig. 7.8). For each rotation, turn the inside circle once so that students can see which centre they are to participate in next.

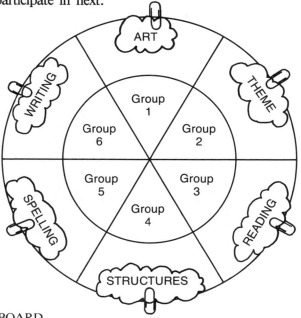

Figure 7.8

EXAMPLE 2

PLANNING BOARD
With a planning board, students move through centres on an individual basis and form self-selected groups. Each student decides the order of activities and the necessary time to complete tasks.

NOTE: To avoid the possible chaos of thirty students approaching the planning board at the same time and then having to wait for their turn to choose, the teacher may assign a short directed activity to be completed prior to choosing a centre at the planning board. Since students will finish the assigned task at different times, they will approach the planning board a few at a time.

a) Write the names of the centres on a board or chart. Students either sign their names beneath the activity in which they choose to participate or move their magnetized name tags under the appropriate column (Fig. 7.9).

Reading	Writing	Math	Puppetry	Structures
Marnie Saul Karen Nadia Mike	Sonya Edson	Kim Matthew Hussein Rena	Aaron Kaari	Mark Naseeb

Figure 7.9

b) Write the centre names (and/or pictures) on the pockets. Student name cards (and/or photos) are placed in the pockets of the centres chosen (Fig. 7.10). Each student may have more than one name card to indicate the day's activities.

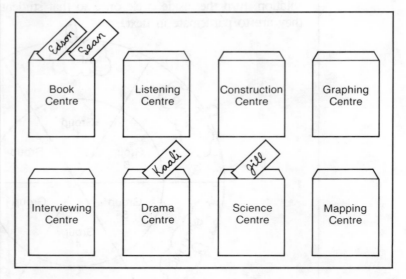

Figure 7.10

c) Write the centre names on the cards. Students place the cards for the centres chosen into their own name pockets (Fig. 7.11). The number of centre cards available indicates the number of students allowed there at a time.

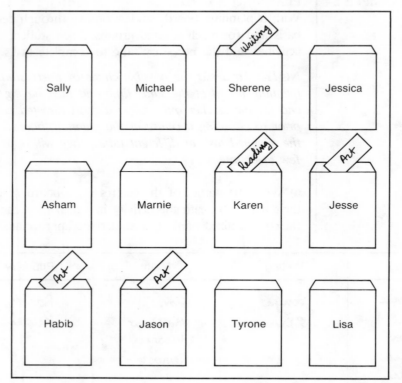

Figure 7.11

d) Write the centre names on cards. The number of pockets beside each centre card indicates the number of students permitted at that centre at one time. Students place their name cards in the pockets for the centre chosen (Fig. 7.12, opposite top).

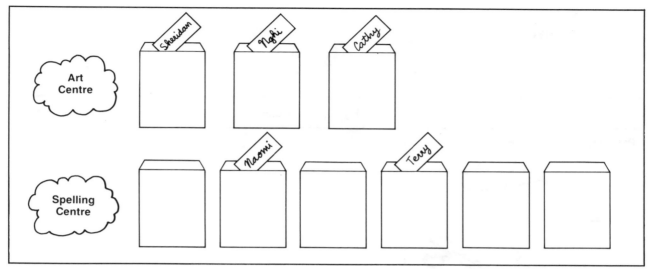

Figure 7.12

e) Write a number on the pocket to indicate the number of students allowed at the centre at any one time. Students move their name cards to the appropriate pockets, but also sign on the sheets below the centre pockets. They put checks beside their names when the work is completed (Fig. 7.13). This type of planning board promotes peer teaching because students who are having difficulties can ask for help from those students who have already completed the task.

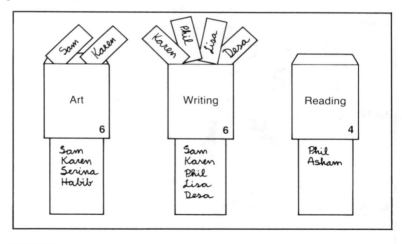

Figure 7.13

EXAMPLE 3

TRACKING SHEETS

Tracking sheets serve as a method of monitoring student movement through activities. Students choose an activity from the tracking sheet and mark the appropriate place when completed. These sheets are kept in desks or personal bins, or are stored in folders, scrapbooks, or notebooks.

Tracking sheets may also be used in conjunction with group rotations or with planning boards because they serve as *records* of student work accomplished. They often include sections for student self-evaluations as well as sections for teacher and/or parent comments.

Figures 7.14 to 7.24 are examples of possible tracking sheets.

a) The tracking sheet in Figure 7.14 (page 66) can be used in two ways. Very young students can simply choose one activity at a time and put a check, sticker, or date stamp in the appropriate box as they begin or complete the activity.

Activities	Monday	Tuesday	Wednesday	Thursday	Friday
Painting 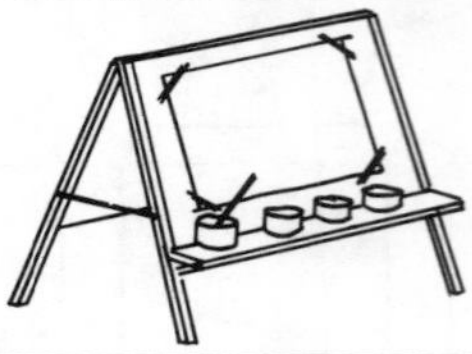			✓		
Cut & Paste 		✓			
Water Table 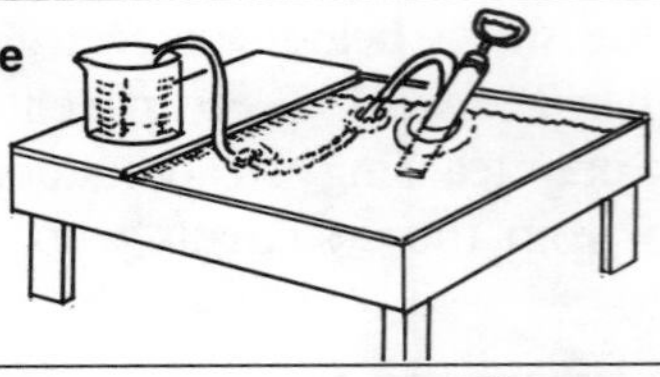			✓		
Home Centre 	✓	✓			
Listening Centre 					
Book Centre 				✓	

Name __Aaron__

The week of __Jan. 9__ to __Jan. 13__

Figure 7.14

For slightly older students, some activities on the tracking sheet can be coded, for example, by star or colour. The students are instructed to alternate between coded and non-coded activities. The coded activities might represent activities that you want all your students to experience. These could be either skill-building or exploratory. Non-coded activities might be reinforcement alternatives.

b) On the tracking sheet in Figure 7.15, students choose their activities and record the name of the centre, the date started and the date completed.

	Centres	Date Started	Date Completed
1.	Math.	Feb. 9	Feb. 9
2.			
3.			
4.			
5.			
6.			

Figure 7.15

c) On the tracking sheet in Figure 7.16, students begin to evaluate their own work and/or behaviour. They use descriptive faces to illustrate how well they think they worked at each centre.

MY TRACKING SHEET	Name Matthew	
Listening Centre	 🙂	Date Mar. 9
Reading Centre	 😐	Mar. 6
Writing Centre	 🙂	Mar. 10
Math Centre		
Art Centre	 🙂	Mar. 5
Odds n' Ends		

Figure 7.16

d) Students can use Figure 7.17 to comment on how well they did at each activity.

Name <u>Daisleon</u>

Centres	Date Started	Date Completed	Comments (Self-evaluation)
1. Music	Mar. 2	Mar. 4	I think my words are coming out much more clearly now.
2. Spelling	Mar. 5		
3.			
4.			
5.			
6.			

Figure 7.17

e) In Figure 7.18, students use a rating scale of 1, 2, or 3 to indicate their accomplishments. Teachers and students can decide whether to rate behaviour, work habits or quality of work.

Name <u>Sopheap</u>

Centres	Date Started	Rate Yourself 1. Wow! 2. Okay. 3. Could be better.
1. Spelling	Feb. 6	2
2. Spelling	Feb. 8	1
3.		
4.		
5.		
6.		

Figure 7.18

f) Figure 7.19 illustrates a distinction between teacher-directed and student-chosen activities. It clearly indicates which activities *must* be done each day and which ones students may choose.

MY TRACKING SHEET		Name **Roy**				
		Date **April 19**				

	Activity	Monday	Tuesday	Wednesday	Thursday	Friday
THINGS I MUST DO	**Reading**	✓	✓	✓		
	Math	✓	✓	✓		
THINGS I WANT TO DO	**Spelling**	✓	✓	✓		
	Writing	✓	✓	✓		
	Printing	✓	✓	✓		
	Art					
	Drama		✓			
	Listening	✓				
	Games & Puzzles			✓		

Figure 7.19

g) The tracking sheet in Figure 7.20 also illustrates musts and wants but applies to a weekly period.

TRACKING SHEET	Name _Tyrone_

MUSTS   Week of _June 13_

√	Choose 10 words, 2 activities
√	Math: 1 arithmetic, 1 measurement, 1 geometry, 1 problem solving
√	Read & make a book jacket
	Finish your interviews/news articles
	Make a want ad or display ad
V	Create a comic strip

WANTS

	Planting activities
	Puppet play with a reporter
	Magnetic board
√	Computer-keyboarding
√	Painting
	Odds n' ends
	Water tub
	Sketching, rubbings
	Audio-visual centre

Figure 7.20

h) The format in Figure 7.21 permits tracking of activities over a lengthy period of time. Students must do the top seven activities, and then can choose the next five.

Name _Debra_		Starting Date _Nov. 10_	

ALL KINDS OF JOBS — MY ACTIVITY CHECKLIST

(Write or stamp the date beside each line when you have completed the activity.)

Activity	Date	My Comment	Teacher's Comment
1. Community walk		This was fun	You set a fine example on our trip — Good Work MC
2. Alphajobs booklet			
3. Interview			
4. Comparative graph			
5. "Roll" model			
6. Earning and spending			
7. When I grow up			
8.			
9.			
10.			
11.			
12.			

Figure 7.21

i) Students can use charts such as Figure 7.22 to keep written records of the tasks to be completed.

Animal Studies	TRACKING SHEET		Name *Sarah*
Centre	**Activity**	**Date Completed**	**Comments**
Theme	Which animals live on land, in water or in air?	Mar. 6	I found that most animals live on land
	Which animals are vertebrates and which are invertebrates?		
	What do they eat? Choose a card and do research.	Mar. 7	I now know that monkeys are omnivores
	Complete the food chain & webs.		
Talking	Sort the buttons/animal pictures/models.	Mar. 4	This was fun
	Tell about your favourite animal.		
Reading	Read an animal fable.		
	Read & tape an animal poem.		
	Find more animal poems.		
Audio-Visual	Listen to an animal story and write at least 3 things you learned.		
	Tape some imaginary animal sounds.	Mar. 5	I got a lot of sounds
	View a filmstrip.		

Figure 7.22

j) The format in Figure 7.23 allows students to record the date, name of centre, and other pertinent information *each* time that they begin work at a centre. Teachers can easily see how much time a student spends at a particular activity. Some students may take many days to complete work at one centre. Others may pass through many centres in one day.

MY TRACKING SHEET

Name _Lyle_

Today's Date	Name of Centre	Description of Each Activity I Worked On or Completed	Comments
Mon. Mar. 6	Diorama Centre	I did Cinderella and the Prince dancing at the ball.	I'm proud of my box.
Mon. Mar. 6	Spelling	I finished my crossword puzzle.	It was fun.
Tues. Mar. 7	Mapping	I started my imaginary map of Hansel and Grettal's trip.	I had trouble starting.
Wed. Mar. 8	Mapping	I'm working on my map.	:-|
Thurs. Mar. 9	Mapping	I finished the map.	I worked hard on it.

Figure 7.23

k) In a log or journal, students can organize and plan their day's accomplishments through writing (Fig. 7.24). They can later reflect on what they have done and teachers can record their comments as well.

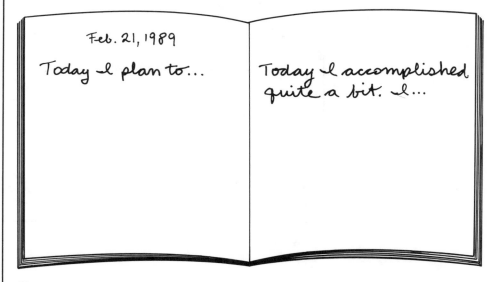

Feb. 21, 1989

Today I plan to...

Today I accomplished quite a bit. I...

Figure 7.24

■ With your students, establish rules, routines, and expectations for the centres.

Promote the following practices:

- working co-operatively with others
- trying to complete work within an acceptable period of time
- being responsible for appropriate use of materials as well as for clean-up
- being responsible for storing and displaying finished and unfinished work
- moving to another self-chosen centre or activity when a task is finished
- keeping tracking sheets up-to-date

■ Closely observe, assess and assist those students who consistently do not complete tasks within an acceptable time frame. A contract can be set up between you and such a student. Involving parents can also be helpful.

Figures 7.25 and 7.26 give examples of student contracts.

EXAMPLE 1

MY CONTRACT

I, _____Stephen_____, will do my best to finish:

_____my research project_____

_____my French story_____

by _____Mon. Jan. 15_____
 (due date)

_____Stephen_____   _____M. Jones._____
Student's Signature   *Teacher's Signature*

Comments: _____

_____

_____

_____

_____   _____
Student's   *Teacher's*
Initials   *Initials*

Figure 7.25

EXAMPLE 2

MY CONTRACT

What I *must* do today...   Math

Spelling

Finish the pictures
for my book

What I *might* do today...   Cut and paste

_____   _____
Student's Signature   Teacher's Signature

Figure 7.26

■ Evaluate and reflect on the child-centred environment you have created.
    Consider these criteria:
• signs and labels
• clear instructions (oral and written)
• concrete manipulative materials
• materials easily accessible to the students
• storage and display areas for materials, resources and student work
• opportunities for active learning—experiencing, interacting, reflecting and communicating
• tasks at varying levels of ability
• open-ended tasks (no right answers)
• student choice of tasks
• opportunities for problem solving and risk taking
• co-operative group learning experiences
• a balance among large group, small group and individual activities
• opportunities for student evaluation and peer evaluation

8

Record Keeping, Student Evaluation and Parental Involvement

Student evaluation is a vital part of programming. Using a combination of evaluative techniques will enable you to meet the programming needs of all your students.

Knowing and understanding where your children are coming from helps you to plan where they are going. Through *diagnostic evaluation* or a needs assessment, you can begin to accumulate data on a child's strengths and/or needs.

Once you have found out what your children already know and you are programming for their needs, you should look at the ongoing processes that they are involved in. *Formative evaluation*, consisting of the collection of ongoing observations and dated work samples over prolonged time periods, forms the basis for modification of programming to meet the individual needs of every child in your classroom. Your observations should be as objective and non-judgmental as possible. Accumulating them will enable you to form interpretations based on recurring and consistently observable behaviours.

You will also need to look at the "product" or the child's ability at a certain point in time. *Summative evaluation* requires you to consider specific work samples, along with student tracking sheets, workbooks and test results. These will give you concrete evidence of progress and are invaluable in discussions with parents and school personnel.

The use of all three of these evaluative measures will help you see where your students are, where they should be going and how to get them there. You will be quite confident and competent in justifying your program to administrative superiors and to parents.

Keeping your parents well informed about their children's educational program helps them to become better able to assist their children at home. They can participate to a much greater extent in their child's physical, social, emotional and cognitive development. Well-informed parents often become the biggest boosters of child-centred classrooms.

Being able to articulate for your parents what you are doing in your classroom and why you are doing it helps them to become more knowledgeable and supportive of your program. Parents from many diverse cultures need to be consciously considered. When providing programming information, newsletters and reports, you should try to offer translations, translators and materials in various languages to meet the needs of the total community.

i) Creating Effective Record-keeping and Student Evaluation Practices

Observing Your Students

■ Observe your students and record objective statements about each student whenever possible during the school day.

You may find the following chart, which considers some aspects of the development of the whole child, helpful in focussing on *what to observe.*

Physical Development
- appearance and behaviours
- large and small motor development
- physical co-ordination
- health and hygiene

Cognitive Development
- predicting and inferring
- solving problems
- making decisions
- understanding cause and effect relationships
- specific skills in all curriculum areas
- different learning styles

Emotional Development
- self-image
- self-confidence
- responsibility
- independence
- coping skills
- stress levels
- organization
- work habits

Social Development
- interactions with peers and with adults
- communicating
- co-operating
- solving problems
- making decisions
- trusting others
- respecting others
- becoming responsible

Recording Your Observations

■ Prepare observation record sheets (Fig. 8.1, page 78).

NOTE: The teacher writes directly onto the paper in the squares, or uses Post-it notes (Fig. 8.2, page 78). These Post-it notes can be placed one on top of the other in the squares as additional observations are made throughout the day or week. In this way, an accumulation of observations about many students are easily stored on one page. These comments should be brief and objective.

OBSERVATION RECORD SHEET

John	Rena	Marnie	Mike
May 3/89 - built 3-D Structure	May 9/89 - Keyboarded by herself		
Aaron	Steve	Phill	Lisa
May 6/89 - wouldn't leave centre until task completed the way he wanted			
Keren	Nadia	Saul	Melissa
Sonya	Phil	Sandi	Kaari

Figure 8.1

This "At a Glance" system of observation and record keeping was introduced in the book Look! Hear! by the North York Board of Education, 1983.

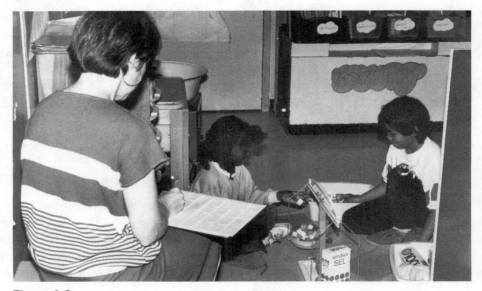

Figure 8.2

- Prepare a summary record sheet for each student (Fig. 8.3). At the end of the week or month, all of the Post-its can be transferred to these one-page summaries.

NOTE: This record-keeping method facilitates report card writing as it ensures that all observations are together.

STUDENT SUMMARY SHEET

Student Name _____ *John* _____	Fall, Winter or Spring Term

Social and Emotional Development	Work Habits *May 16 needed 3 reminders to settle down*

Language *May 7 Used descriptive words in space story*	Mathematics

Drama	Visual Arts	Music	Physical Education Health Education

Social Studies	Science *Sept 3 Built 3-D Structure*

French	Computer *Sept 9 Able to use story-writer word pro.*

Figure 8.3

■ Decide on other evaluation and recording methods to use. Figures 8.4 to 8.7 are possible examples.

EXAMPLE 1

CHECKLIST FOR COMPLETED ACTIVITIES Names of Students	Centres						Comments
	Structure	*Math*	*Diorama*				
Tina	✓	✓	✓				Motivated Enthusiastic!
Larry		✓					Had difficulty with regrouping.
Jason	✓						
Barry			✓				

Figure 8.4

EXAMPLE 2

The checklist in Figure 8.5 opposite is not intended to list concepts that need to be taught. It is intended to build your awareness of the kinds of things students may be exhibiting in their writing. You can use it to understand a student's developmental stage in writing at a particular time and to look at a piece of writing in a more knowledgeable way. Once you know *what* a particular student is doing in writing, you will be better able to meet the needs of that student through your programming.

OBSERVING CHILDREN'S WRITING

CONTENT

Type of Writing
- [ ] Expressive
- [ ] Transactional
- [x] Poetic

Maturity
- [ ] Egocentric
- [ ] Bed-to-bed pattern
- [ ] Awareness of others
- [x] Awareness of audience

Development of Story Line
- [x] A beginning
- [x] A middle
- [x] An ending
- [x] Sufficient information
- [x] Well developed
- [x] Unity of thought
- [x] Smooth flow of ideas

Organization
- [x] Coherent
- [x] Logical
- [x] Sequential
- [x] Suits the purpose of the writing

Language
- [x] Appropriate to the writing
- [ ] Use of descriptive words
- [x] Use of conversation
- [ ] Use of metaphors
- [ ] Use of similes

Interest
- [x] Holds audience's attention
- [x] Imaginative
- [ ] Humorous
- [ ] Repetition for effect

MECHANICS

Grammar and Usage
- [ ] Sentence fragments
- [x] Complete sentences
- [ ] Run-on sentences
- [x] Short sentences
- [x] Subject-verb agreement
- [ ] Use of conjunctions
- [ ] Use of adjectives
- [ ] Use of adverbs
- [ ] Use of clauses
- [ ] Use of adverbial clauses

Capitalization
- [x] Beginning of sentences
- [x] Proper names

Punctuation
- [x] Use of periods
- [x] Use of question marks
- [x] Use of exclamation marks
- [x] Use of quotation marks
- [ ] Use of commas

Spelling
- [ ] Use of scribble
- [ ] Use of random letters
- [ ] Use of initial consonants
- [ ] Use of phonetic spelling
- [x] Use of conventional spelling with few errors
- [x] Use of plurals
- [x] Use of endings (-ed, -ing, -tion)

Figure 8.5

The mistery of
The Trap Door!
chapter 1
The trap door

Once apoun a time there were two girls
named Kim and Hila. One day they
went to the park. When they got there
they started to play. Just then Hila
saw something. "Come here Kim". Said
Hila "What do you want"? Said Kim
"I found a trap door right here".

Figure 8.6

EXAMPLE 3

On the writing conference sheet in Figure 8.7, you can summarize what was discussed during a conference with one of your students. The "Issues Discussed" section might pertain to either the *content* or *mechanics* of the student's writing. The "Follow-up" section encourages you to devise teaching strategies for use with that particular student.

```
┌──────────────────────────────────────────────────────────┐
│            WRITING CONFERENCE SHEET                        │
│                                                           │
│  Name  Rena                    Date  Nov 10/89            │
│                                                           │
│  Type of Writing  poetic-storywriting                     │
│                        (expressive, transactional, poetic)│
│  Subject of Writing  Julie gets on the "Price is Right"   │
│                                                           │
│  Type of Conference  editing mechanics                    │
│           (choosing a topic, storytelling, drafting,      │
│                          revising, editing, publishing)   │
│  Issues Discussed  use of quotation marks                 │
│                                                           │
│  Follow-up  point out books using dialogue                │
│   and note quotation marks; observe                       │
│   further writing to see if any transfer                  │
│   occurs.                                                 │
│                                                           │
└──────────────────────────────────────────────────────────┘
```

Figure 8.7

■ Collect and store dated samples of your students' work.
  The following are examples of individual filing systems:

- theme folders
- writing folders
- art portfolios
- hanging files
- file box
- scrapbook
- envelopes
- logbook
- notebook

■ Write in-depth anecdotal notes about each student on a regular basis.

Using Your Observations

■ Examine all the relevant data that you have collected on each student. Look for patterns of behaviour and evidence of growth.

■ In collecting information about each student, you may want to consult parents/guardians, school files, other teachers, social service workers, the school nurse, and/or support staff.

- Make inferences and judgements based on a student's progress and behaviour patterns.

- Adjust your program to ensure that you meet the needs of individual students.

- Using the collected data, write clear, concise evaluative statements for reporting purposes.

    The following sample comments may assist you in report card writing.

General Comments
- is gaining steadily in self-confidence
- aspires to higher levels of sophistication
- produces high calibre work
- responds well to reassurances and constructive criticisms
- derives enjoyment from...
- continues to apply himself/herself to...
- shows increased self-confidence in...
- enjoys a challenge in...
- rises to the challenges presented
- contributes many original ideas
- displays creativity and imagination in...
- her/his enthusiasm are noteworthy attributes
- her/his leadership qualities are an asset
- is developing good work habits both in directed and independent situations
- functions extremely well in group situations
- is aware of the importance of...
- is aware of the benefits of...
- is quick to grasp new ideas
- assumes a responsible approach to...
- an encouraging sign lately has been...
- is improving in his/her ability to...
- it would be most beneficial for...to....
- has not yet realized his/her potential in....
- has developed some better work habits but is not always consistent in their application
- a more consistent effort is necessary
- at times, forgets the importance of good independent work habits
- needs encouragement and reinforcement in....
- is easily discouraged
- is experiencing difficulty in working in group situations
- is slow to begin assignments
- needs encouragement to complete assignments
- is less comfortable in creative situations
- rarely becomes voluntarily involved in discussions
- is easily distracted
- needs more reminders to stay on task and not disturb others around him/her
- is being encouraged to pay close attention to instructions
- is working on...
- is being encouraged to put more thought and effort into his/her daily assignments

---

Mathematics

- grasps mathematical concepts easily
- has a good grasp of the concepts covered in math this term, for example...
- enjoys a challenge in this area
- applies the operations she/he has learned to solving problems
- is competent in reasoning things out to a logical conclusion
- has difficulty in grasping new concepts
- displays uncertainty when faced with new concepts but overcomes it with time and encouragement
- needs much reinforcement in grasping new concepts
- is working at improving the speed and accuracy of her/his number work
- has the ability to retain information and recall it when needed
- uses mathematical language appropriately
- illustrates new learning in a variety of ways
- is able to recognize and name solid shapes
- shows good understanding of geometric concepts
- is able to easily add and subtract two-digit numerals
- has a sound understanding of quantity and measure
- is able to tell time with confidence

Language

- is aware of the benefits of independent reading
- enjoys reading orally
- oral reading displays fluency and good expression
- participates well in shared reading experiences
- can use all cueing systems when faced with unfamiliar words or passages
- readily/frequently chooses reading as an independent activity
- makes use of phonetic skills and picture clues
- shows understanding of material read
- is able to predict and infer
- is able to extract information and meaning from what she/he reads
- is able to decode words but is experiencing some difficulty in understanding the meaning of passages
- does not readily choose reading as an independent activity
- enjoys choosing own topics for story writing
- bases writing on personal experiences
- has a good awareness of audience
- is able to organize his/her thoughts in a clear and concise manner
- shows clarity of thought in written work
- uses humour in stories written
- I am enjoying his/her creative attempts at writing
- enjoys taking written work to published form
- shows pride in his/her published efforts
- needs encouragement and reassurance in choosing own topics for story writing
- has a great many stories to tell but has difficulty putting them into written form
- contributions in oral discussions are worthwhile and well expressed
- can originate ideas which he/she readily shares with others
- listens carefully and is considerate of the opinions of others
- oral contributions are often unrelated to the topic being discussed
- needs many reminders to listen carefully while others are speaking
- does not readily participate in group discussions

Environmental Studies
- demonstrates a good background knowledge
- is able to observe and make predictions
- participates enthusiastically in all activities
- participates well in group investigations
- has satisfactorily completed all of the assigned tasks for our unit on....
- is to be commended for his/her efforts in our studies of....
- is very aware and interested in her/his environment
- is curious and observes the world around him/her
- discusses intelligently
- needs encouragement to complete assignments in....
- experiences difficulty in organizing information
- uses equipment and tools appropriately, for example, microscope, audio-visual materials

The Arts
- enjoys participating in all areas of the Arts
- expresses feelings and thoughts through artistic attempts
- artwork shows good small muscle co-ordination
- pays attention to detail
- uses a wide variety of materials in creative attempts
- demonstrates a particular flair for dramatics
- has enjoyed participating in the Choir this term
- sings with enthusiasm
- enjoys musical activities
- shows an awareness of rhythm and beat in musical activities
- participates fully/enthusiastically in all aspects of our gym program
- demonstrates good large muscle co-ordination
- shows originality and creativity in....
- is flexible and agile
- is well co-ordinated
- follows instructions well and plays safely
- strives to improve athletic performance
- is encouraged to put more thought into her/his artistic endeavours
- puts a minimum amount of effort into his/her....
- requires continued encouragement to co-operate in gym class
- must remember to bring gym clothes every day
- is urged to display better sportsmanship

ii) Creating and Improving Parental Involvement

■ Make an initial contact with all parents early in the school year by scheduling a curriculum night or information meeting, writing a letter or newsletter, or telephoning. Introduce yourself and outline clear program objectives and expectations.

■ Keep parents regularly informed about school activities and programs. They will be better able to discuss and reinforce school activities with their children. You may find the sample letters in Figures 8.8 to 8.14 helpful.

EXAMPLE 1 | The letter in Figure 8.8 outlines the focus of study for the term and prepares parents for several upcoming trips.

Dear Parent or Guardian

Our class will be studying the Community in our first social studies unit this term. We will begin by investigating our own neighbourhood and will later focus on the larger community of North York.

We will be going on several neighbourhood walks, as well as a bus trip to the North York City Hall.

This study will develop and strengthen your child's mapping, interviewing, tallying, graphing, researching, and reporting skills, among others.

More specific information on trips and outings will be forwarded to you later.

Sincerely

S. Schwartz

S Schwartz

Figure 8.8

EXAMPLE 2 | The letter in Figure 8.9 outlines information about classroom programming already completed.

Dear Parent or Guardian

Our class has completed an environmental studies unit on animal groupings. This unit illustrated to the children that all living things are dependent on each other for their survival. It included such activities as sorting and classifying animals into various groups, researching animal eating habits, and constructing box sculptures that illustrated different animal habitats and food chains.

The children enjoyed taking part in this unit of study and are now looking forward to sharing their work with you.

Sincerely

M. Pollishuke

M Pollishuke

Figure 8.9

EXAMPLE 3 | The letter in Figure 8.10 explains the concept of learning centres to parents.

Dear Parent or Guardian

Throughout the school year, your child may mention his/her involvement in "learning centres."

In our classroom, "learning centres" are planned around various themes or curriculum areas. These centres encourage the developing physical, social, emotional and intellectual needs of the children. When taking part in these centres, your child will have many opportunities to work with a group, to develop and strengthen the understanding of concepts and skills, to make decisions, and to solve problems.

Interaction with their fellow students and between teacher and students at centres promotes co-operation--an essential life skill--and makes for valuable and positive learning experiences.

Attached to this letter is a list of the centres that your child will be taking part in this term.

If you have any questions, please call me at the school at 769-2222.

Sincerely

S. Schwartz

S Schwartz

Figure 8.10

EXAMPLE 4 | The letter in Figure 8.11 provides information about the language focus in the classroom. It can be useful as a starting point for discussion on a curriculum night or during interview sessions.

Dear Parent or Guardian

I would like to outline some of the language learning experiences that your child will have this year.

SPEAKING
There will be daily opportunities for your child to express questions, ideas and opinions, in large group discussions, with a partner, and with adults. These opportunities are designed to encourage communication skills.

LISTENING
Listening carefully is an important part of our language program. Children must learn to listen carefully in order to learn new facts and ideas and to understand instructions and directions. Developing listening skills will be emphasized in large and small group discussions, and also at our audio-visual centre.

READING
Research has proven that children learn to read by reading. The more they read and discuss what they read, the better readers they will become. Our focus is to encourage children to read for meaning, to understand what they are reading, and to read more fluently. To reach this goal, the children will take part in many reading activities throughout the day.

I hope that you will encourage your child to read at home and that you or another adult will read to him/her daily.

WRITING
The writing program this year emphasizes daily writing and a sense of authorship. The children will be involved in much the same activities as real authors. They will

    . discuss their ideas
    . talk out their stories
    . write draft copies
    . share their stories
    . change and revise/rework selected stories
    . edit and publish selected stories

..../2

Figure 8.11

Page 2

When the children first write their stories, I encourage them to write all the letters they hear and not to worry about correct spelling at first. In this way, their thoughts will flow freely onto paper. The students will be revising or changing selected pieces of their writing. When they prepare to share their work with others, they see the need for correct spelling, punctuation and grammar. When they publish their writing, they gain confidence and pride in their accomplishments.

I hope that you will encourage your child to write often at home. I would welcome sharing any home writing at school.

SPELLING
The children's spelling skills will improve as they read, write and experiment with words. Research has shown that children must feel free to try different spellings before they become competent spellers. They will be working with words from their own writing and from their theme studies.

MUSIC
The music program will also emphasize language. Children read and learn new words to a variety of new songs and sing for enjoyment. The music program will also involve experimenting with sound, rhythm, and movement.

I hope to communicate with you frequently. Please get in touch with me if you have any questions or concerns (call the school at 769-2222).

Sincerely

M. Pollishuke

M Pollishuke

Figure 8.11 cont'd

■ Provide parents with concrete examples of how they can help their children at home.

EXAMPLE 1 | The letter in Figure 8.12 provides ideas about how parents can help children with *reading* at home.

Dear Parent or Guardian

The following suggestions are some practical ideas for you to use to encourage your child to read at home.

. Set up a shelf with his/her favourite books.
. Make regular trips to the library.
. Ask the librarian to recommend good books.
. Give books as gifts.
. Let your child see you read. Children learn by imitating.
. Read and share books and stories with your child regularly in the language you are most comfortable with.
. Establish a regular daily reading time, for example, after supper or before bedtime.
. Relate reading to everyday life situations (billboards, traffic signs, menus, TV guides, catalogues, labels, maps, etc.).

Thank you for your continuing interest and support.

Sincerely

S Schwartz

S Schwartz

Figure 8.12

EXAMPLE 2 | The letter in Figure 8.13 outlines ideas on how parents can help children with *writing* at home.

Dear Parent or Guardian

As you know, learning to write effectively is a very important part of your child's education. Here are some practical ideas on how you can help your child with writing at home.

- Let your child see you write often. Show that writing is a purposeful, real-life activity.
- Leave your child notes (in lunch boxes, under pillows) and encourage him/her to write back.
- Encourage your child to help in writing out shopping lists, birthday cards, invitations, etc.
- Purchase a diary and suggest that your child make daily entries.
- Encourage your child to write letters. Help her/him find a pen pal.
- Have paper, pencils, markers, etc., available to encourage writing at home.
- Find a place in your home for writing or doing school work.
- Whenever possible, take your child on outings such as to shopping malls, museums, planetariums, art displays, concerts, sporting events, an airport, a farm, city hall, a zoo, amusement parks, and family vacations. These enriching experiences will be possible topics for your child's writing.
- Discuss possible ideas for writing with your child.
- Be an audience for your child's ideas.

Thank you for your continuing interest and support.

Sincerely

M. Pollishuke

M Pollishuke

Figure 8.13

EXAMPLE 3 The letter in Figure 8.14 suggests ways in which parents can help children develop a positive attitude towards school and learning.

Dear Parent or Guardian

Here are some practical suggestions for how you can help your child do well in school and enjoy learning.

. Let your child explore and experiment with materials, toys and "hands-on" activities such as building with blocks, typing, cooking, and sewing. Children learn best by <u>doing</u>.

. Take advantage of daily learning situations to point out colours, numbers, letters and words. Count the number of plates on the table, talk about the colours in the striped shirt she/he is wearing, read and discuss prices during shopping outings, etc.

. Oversee the type of television programs your child watches and control how much time he/she spends watching. Discuss the programs with your child and make television a shared experience.

. Let your child be responsible for some household chore.

. Let your child make decisions by giving him/her choice in such matters as breakfast food, birthday celebrations, bedroom colour, clothing, etc.

. Seek out your child's strengths and capabilities and praise her/him whenever possible.

. Play games with your child that require concentration. Often such games can help to increase problem-solving and thinking skills.

. Have good conversations with your child and ask thought-provoking questions. Listen actively.

Thank you for your continuing interest and support.

Sincerely

S Schwartz

S Schwartz

Figure 8.14

■ Provide opportunities for parents to participate in school or classroom events.
   Here are some examples of what parents can do:

- supervise class trips
- type students' stories
- help with the editing and publishing of students' writing
- act as parent volunteers in the classroom or library
- join Home and School associations
- present topics in which they have particular strengths
- be interviewed about their occupations
- help organize fun fairs, conferences for young authors, etc.

■ Provide interested parents with opportunities to read educational documents and resources to promote a better understanding of current philosophy and practices. Set up a lending library for parents to borrow your resource books or educational videotapes.
   (Refer to the Bibliography on page 98 for a list of resources.)

■ Make contact with individual parents on a *regular* basis—not merely to discuss a child's background experiences, programs and problems, but to celebrate successes.

■ During interviews with parents, reinforce the idea of a *team effort* between home and school. You and your parents need to work together to provide the best possible education for your students. Discuss the child's progress. Examine and discuss dated work samples, informal and/or formal test results, daily observations, and your interpretations. Answer questions about your program and about report card comments. Be positive and encouraging.
   The checklist in Figure 8.15 may prove helpful to you.

A CHECKLIST FOR SUCCESSFUL PARENT INTERVIEWS

☑ **Be Prepared to Discuss:**
- Purpose of interview
- Key issues
- Student Work Samples
- Records
- Background information
- Suggestions for parents

☑ **Start and Finish on Time**

☑ **Be Positive**
- Focus on strengths
- Work as a team with parents

☑ **Be Encouraging**
- Praise when appropriate

☑ **Be an Active Listener**

☑ **Be Confident**

☑ **Be Professional and Avoid Discussing**
- Other children
- Experiences with other teachers
- Other teachers' programs

☑ **Show Appreciation to Parents**
- For being present
- For being interested
- For being involved

☑ **Be Yourself!**

Figure 8.15

Conclusion

The child-centred classroom works! We have tried it, and we have seen the results. Our students have become independent, self-motivated decision makers and problem solvers. But above all else, they are excited about learning. This book is our attempt to help you experience that excitement.

Since people learn to do by doing, the true test and value of this book will occur when you begin to act upon the practical suggestions and experiment with some of the many activities. You will experience for yourself the child-centred classroom. You will see and understand the obvious benefits to both your students and yourself. You will begin to modify, adapt, and adjust the book's ideas to your own specific strengths, needs and interests.

It is important to understand that the transformation your classroom will undergo will be gradual. Creating a child-centred classroom often requires us to dramatically change our ideas about how children learn and how teachers teach. This change of underlying beliefs does not happen overnight. Everyone needs time to adjust to a new philosophy, a changed environment, increased activity, and the greater enthusiasm towards learning that will inevitably emerge as children interact with varied materials and with each other at different work spaces around the classroom.

Keep in mind that you need to continue to refine your ideas and practices, to continue to do, to try, and to grow personally and professionally. And keep in mind, too, that creating the child-centred classroom is indeed a possibility!

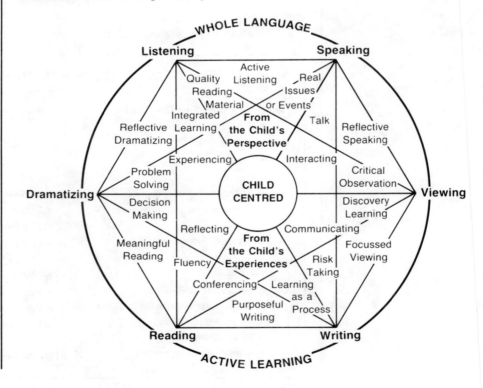

Appendix
Favourite Children's Books

** Starred books are excellent examples for **patterning**.*

Poetry

Alligator Pie*, Dennis Lee (Macmillan, 1974)

Auntie's Knitting a Baby, Lois Simmie (Western Producer, 1984)

Butterscotch Dreams*, Sonja Dunn (Pembroke, 1987)

Chicken Soup with Rice*, Maurice Sendak (Harper & Row, 1962)

Giraffe and a Half, Shel Silverstein (Harper & Row, 1964)

Golden Unicorn, Phyllis A. Whitney (Fawcett, 1985)

If I Found a Wistful Unicorn*, Ann Ashford (Peachtree, 1978)

Jelly Belly, Dennis Lee (Macmillan, 1983)

A Light in the Attic, Shel Silverstein (Harper & Row, 1981)

Mischief City, Tim Wynne-Jones (Groundwood, 1986)

Nightmares: Poems to Trouble Your Sleep, Jack Prelutsky (Greenwillow Books, 1976)

Scary Poems for Rotten Kids, Sean O'Huigin (Black Moss, 1988)

Toes in My Nose, Sheree Fitch (Doubleday, 1987)

Where the Sidewalk Ends, Shel Silverstein (Harper & Row, 1974)

Picture Books

Alexander and the Terrible, Horrible, No Good, Very Bad Day*, Judith Viorst (Macmillan, 1987)

Ape in a Cape*, Fritz Eichenberg (Harcourt, Brace Jovanovich, 1973)

Balloon Tree, Phoebe Gilman (Scholastic, 1984)

Big or Little*, Kathy Stinson (Annick Press, 1985)

Brown Bear, Brown Bear, What Do You See?*, Bill Martin, Jr. (Holt, Henry, 1983)

Boss for a Week*, Libby Handy (Scholastic, 1984)

The Boy in the Drawer, Robert Munsch (Annick Press, 1986)

Bread and Jam for Frances, Russell Hoban (Harper & Row, 1986)

The Carrot Seed, Ruth Krauss (Harper & Row, 1945)

The Caterpillar and the Polliwog, Jack Kent (Prentice-Hall, 1982)

Chin Chiang and the Dragon's Dance, Ian Wallace (Groundwood, 1984)

Corduroy, Don Freeman (Viking Press, 1968)

Dear Zoo*, Rod Campbell (Penguin, 1987)

Each Peach Pear Plum*, Janet and Allan Ahlberg (Scholastic, 1985)

From Me to You, Paul Rogers (Orchard Books, 1987)

Fortunately*, Remy Charlip (Macmillan, 1985)

Free Fall, David Wiesner (Lothrop, Lee & Shepard, 1988)

A Forest of Dreams, Rosemary Wells and Susan Jeffers (Dial Books, 1988)

The Giving Tree, Shel Silverstein (Harper & Row, 1964)

Goggles, Ezra Jack Keats (Collier, 1971)

Goodnight, Moon, Margaret W. Brown (Harper & Row, 1977)

Good Times, Bad Times*, Harold Evans (Atheneum, 1984)

Good Times, Bad Times, Mummy and Me, Priscilla Galloway (Women's Press, 1980)

The Hating Book*, Charlotte Zolotow (Harper & Row, 1969)

A House Is a House for Me*, Mary Ann Hoberman (Viking Press, 1978)

How Much Is a Million?, David M. Schwartz (Scholastic, 1987)

How to Get Rid of Bad Dreams*, Nancy Hazbry and Roy Condy (Scholastic, 1983)

I Can Blink*, Frank Asch (Crown, 1986)

I Don't Mind Being Short*, Slavica Popadic (Black Moss, 1986)

I Have to Go!, Robert Munsch (Annick Press, 1987)

If I Were in Charge of the World...and Other Worries*, Judith Viorst (Macmillan, 1984)

Jim and the Beanstalk, Raymond Briggs (Putnam, 1980)

The Jolly Postman*, Janet and Allan Ahlberg (Little, 1986)

Jumanji, Chris Van Allsburg (Houghton Mifflin, 1981)

Just Me and My Dad*, Mercer Mayer (Western, 1977)

Just for You*, Mercer Mayer (Western, 1975)

Knots on a Counting Rope, Bill Martin, Jr., and John Archambault (Holt, Henry, 1987)

Leo the Late Bloomer, Robert Kraus (Harper & Row, 1987)

Little Bear, Else H. Minarik (Harper & Row, 1978)

Longest Journey in the World*, E.M. Forster (Knopf, 1922)

Love You Forever, Robert Munsch (Firefly, 1986)

Mary of Mile 18, Ann Blades (Tundra Books, 1988)

Millicent and the Wind, Robert Munsch (Annick Press, 1984)

Ming Lo Moves the Mountain, Arnold Lobel (Scholastic, 1986)

Miss Nelson Is Missing*, Harry Allard (Scholastic, 1978)

Miss Rumphius, Barbara Cooney (Penguin, 1985)

Mud Puddle, Robert Munsch (Annick Press, 1981)

Murmel, Murmel, Murmel, Robert Munsch (Annick Press, 1982)

My Mama Says There Aren't Any Zombies, Ghosts, etc.*, Judith Viorst (Macmillan, 1977)

Noisy Nora, Rosemary Wells (Dial Books for Young Readers, 1980)

The North Wind & the Sun, La Fontaine (Oxford Press, 1964)

The Old Woman & Her Pig & Ten Other Stories, Anne Rockwell, (Harper & Row, 1979)

Over in the Meadow, Olive A. Wadsworth (Scholastic, 1985)

The Paperbag Princess, Robert Munsch (Annick Press, 1981)

Pigs, Robert Munsch (Annick Press, 1989)

The Polar Express, Chris Van Allsburg (Houghton Mifflin, 1985)

A Promise Is a Promise, Robert Munsch (Annick Press, 1988)

The Queen Who Stole the Sky, Jennifer Garrett (Scholastic, 1986)

The Rainbow Goblins, Ul de Rico (Warner Books, 1979)

Red Is Best*, Kathy Stinson (Annick Press, 1982)

A Rose in My Garden*, Anita and Arnold Lobel (Scholastic, 1985)

Rosie's Walk, Pat Hutchins (Macmillan, 1981)

The Shrinking of Treehorn, Florence Parry Heide (Holiday House, 1971)

Sign on Rosie's Door, Maurice Sendak (Harper & Row, 1984)

The Snowman, Raymond Briggs (Puffin Books, 1988)

Someday*, Charlotte Zolotow (Harper & Row, 1965)

Stone Soup, Ann McGovern (Scholastic)

Summer Is..., Charlotte Zolotow (Harper & Row, 1983)

Sylvester and the Magic Pebble, William Steig (Windmill, 1969)

Those Green Things*, Kathy Stinson (Annick Press, 1985)

Tikki Tikki Tembo, Arlene Mosel (Scholastic, 1972)

Today Was a Terrible Day*, Patricia R. Giff (Penguin, 1984)

The Velveteen Rabbit, Margery Williams (Scholastic, 1988)

The Very Hungry Caterpillar, Eric Carle (Philomel Books, 1981)

Where Does the Butterfly Go When It Rains? May Garelick (Scholastic, 1970)
Where the Wild Things Are, Maurice Sendak (Harper & Row, 1984)
Wilfrid Gordon McDonald Partridge, Mem Fox (Penguin, 1984)
Would You Rather . . . *, John Burningham (Harper & Row, 1984)
A Writer, M.B. Goffstein (Harper & Row, 1984)
Zoom at Sea, Tim Wynne-Jones (Groundwood, 1983)

Alphabet Word Books

Animalia*, Graeme Base (Irwin, 1987)
Book of Terns*, Peter Delacorte and Michael Witte (Penguin, 1978)
Don't Cross Your Bridges*, Judith Frost Stark (Price/Stern/Sloan, 1985)
Eight Ate: A Feast of Homonym Riddles*, Marvin Terban (Clarion, 1982)
Faint Frogs Feeling Feverish*, Lillian Obligado (Penguin, 1986)
Father Foxes Pennyrhymes, Clyde Watson (Harper & Row, 1987)
A Northern Alphabet, Ted Harrison (Tundra Books, 1987)
Priceless Proverbs*, Judith Stark (Price/Stern/Sloan, 1982)
Q Is for Duck*, Mary Elting and Michael Folson (Houghton Mifflin, 1980)

Novels

A Bear Called Paddington, Michael Bond (Collins, 1958)
A Boy of Taché, Ann Blades (Tundra Books, 1984)
Bridge to Terabithia, Katherine Paterson (Crowell, 1977)
Charlie and the Chocolate Factory, Roald Dahl (Puffin, 1988)
Charlotte's Web, E.B. White (Harper & Row, 1952)
Dear Mr. Henshaw, Beverly Cleary (Dell, 1984)
From Anna, Jean Little (Fitzhenry & Whiteside, 1977)
Haunted House, Peggy Parish (Dell, 1981)
Hey World, Here I Am!, Jean Little (Kids Can, 1986)
The Hobbit, J.R.R. Tolkien (Methuen, 1966)
Jacob Two-Two Meets the Hooded Fang, Mordecai Richler (Bantam, 1987)
James and the Giant Peach, Roald Dahl (Bantam, 1981)
Julie of the Wolves, Jean C. George (Harper & Row, 1972)
Keeper of the Isis Light, Monica Hughes (Macmillan, 1981)
The Lion, the Witch and the Wardrobe, C.S. Lewis (Macmillan, 1981)
Little House in the Big Woods, Laura Ingalls Wilder (Harper & Row, 1986)
The Mouse & the Motorcycle, Beverly Cleary (Scholastic, 1988)
The Olden Days Coat, Margaret Laurence (McClelland & Stewart, 1979)
The One in the Middle Is the Green Kangaroo, Judy Blume (Dell, 1982)
Otherwise Known as Sheila the Great, Judy Blume (Dell, 1986)
Owls in the Family, Farley Mowat (McClelland & Stewart, 1980)
Pippi Longstocking, Astrid Lindgren (Penguin, 1977)
Ramona the Pest, Beverly Cleary (Dell, 1982)
The Root Cellar, Janet Lunn (Penguin, 1983)
The Secret Garden, Frances H. Burnett (Scholastic, 1987)
Stone Fox, John Reynolds Gardiner (Harper & Row, 1983)
Stuart Little, E.B. White (Harper & Row, 1945)
The Summer of the Swans, Betsy Byars (Avon, 1980)
Sweetgrass, Jan Hudson (Tree Frog, 1984)
Tales of a Fourth Grade Nothing, Judy Blume (Dell, 1976)
Tuck Everlasting, Natalie Babbitt (Bantam, 1976)
Winnie the Pooh, A.A. Milne (Methuen, 1926)
A Wrinkle in Time, Madelaine L'Engle (Dell, 1976)

Bibliography

Atwell, Nancie. *In the Middle: Writing, Reading and Learning with Adolescents.* Portsmouth, New Hampshire: Boynton/Cook, 1987.

Barton, Bob. *Tell Me Another.* Markham, Ontario: Pembroke Publishers, 1986.

Butler, Andrea, and Turbill, Jan. *Towards a Reading-Writing Classroom.* Portsmouth, New Hampshire: Heinemann Educational Books, 1987.

Calkins, Lucy McCormick. *The Art of Teaching Writing.* Portsmouth, New Hampshire: Heinemann Educational Books, 1986.

Calkins, Lucy McCormick. *Lessons from a Child.* Portsmouth, New Hampshire: Heinemann Educational Books, 1983.

Clay, Marie M. *Observing Young Readers: Selected Papers.* Portsmouth, New Hampshire: Heinemann Educational Books, 1982.

Clay, Marie M. *What Did I Write?* Auckland, New Zealand: Heinemann Educational Books, 1975.

Dishon, Dee, and Wilson, Pat. *A Guidebook for Co-operative Learning: A Technique for Creating More Effective Schools.* Portage, Michigan: Cooperation Unlimited, 1984.

Frank, Marjorie. *If You're Trying to Teach Kids to Write, You've Gotta Have This Book.* Nashville, Tennessee: Incentive Publications, 1979.

Gentry, J. Richard. *Spel...Is a Four Letter Word.* Richmond Hill, Ontario: Scholastic-TAB Publications, 1986.

Goodman, Kenneth S. *What's Whole in Whole Language?* Richmond Hill, Ontario: Scholastic-TAB Publications, 1986.

Graves, Donald. *Donald Graves in Australia: "Children Want to Write...".* Rozell, New South Wales: Primary English Teaching Association, 1983.

Graves, Donald. *Writing: Teachers and Children at Work.* Portsmouth, New Hampshire: Heinemann Educational Books, 1983.

Heald-Taylor, Gail. *Whole Language Learning for ESL Students.* Toronto: OISE Press, 1986.

Johnson, David W. and Johnson, Roger T. *Structuring Cooperative Learning: Lesson Plans for Teachers.* New Brighton, Minnesota: Interaction Book Co., 1984.

Kaplan, Sandra Nina. *Change for Children, Ideas and Activities for Individualizing Learning.* Santa Monica, California: Goodyear Publishing, 1973.

Malloch, Jean and Ian. *Books Alive.* Toronto: Doubleday Publishers, 1986.

Malloch, Jean. *Chime In.* Toronto: Doubleday Publishers, 1981.

Metropolitan Toronto School Board. *Together We Learn.* Toronto: Metropolitan Toronto School Board, 1988.

Moorman, Chick, and Dishon, Dee. *Our Classroom: We Can Learn Together.* Revised Edition. Portage, Michigan: The Institute for Personal Power, 1986.

Napier-Anderson, Lois. *Change: One Step at a Time.* Toronto: University of Toronto Guidance Centre, 1981.

Newman, Judith. *The Craft of Children's Writing.* Richmond Hill, Ontario: Scholastic-TAB Publications, 1984.

Newman, Judith. *Whole Language: Theory in Use.* Portsmouth, New Hampshire: Heinemann Educational Books, 1985.

Norris, D. and Bouchard, J. *Observing Children.* Toronto: Toronto Board of Education, 1980.

North York Board of Education, Curriculum and Staff Development Services. *Active Learning, Teaching and Learning in the Junior Division.* North York: North York Board of Education, 1987.

North York Board of Education, Curriculum and Staff Development Services. *Look! Hear! Developing Programs for Primary Children Based on Observations of Learning Needs.* North York: North York Board of Education, 1983.

Ontario Ministry of Education and Ontario Public School Teachers' Federation. *Ages 9 Through 12: A Resource Book for Teachers, a Support Document to The Formative Years.* Toronto: Ontario Ministry of Education and Ontario Public School Teacher's Federation, 1986.

Ontario Ministry of Education. *Education in the Primary and Junior Divisions.* Toronto: Ontario Ministry of Education, 1975.

Ontario Ministry of Education. *The Formative Years.* Toronto: Ontario Ministry of Education, 1975.

Ontario Ministry of Education. *Shared Discovery.* Toronto: Ontario Ministry of Education, 1980.

Schwartz, Susan. *All Write: A Teacher's Guide to Writing, K-6.* Toronto: OISE Press, 1987.

Smith, Frank. *Insult to Intelligence.* Portsmouth, New Hampshire: Heinemann Educational Books, 1986.

Trelease, Jim. *The Read-Aloud Handbook*, Revised Edition. Markham, Ontario: Penguin Books, 1985.

Wells, Gordon. *The Meaning Makers.* Portsmouth, New Hampshire: Heinemann Educational Books, 1986.

Whole Language Consultants. *Reading, Writing and Caring.* Winnipeg, Manitoba: Whole Language Consultants Ltd., 1985.

Blackline Masters

For Student Use

BL	1	Student Evaluation Sheet
BL	2	Student Evaluation Sheet
BL	3	Student Contract
BL	4	Student Contract
BL	5	Student Reading Record Sheet
BL	6	Student Writing Record Sheet
BL	7	Student Planning Sheet
BL	8 - BL 13	Student Tracking Sheets

For Teacher Use

BL	14	Teacher Procedure Planning Sheet
BL	15	Teacher Learning Centre Checklist
BL	16	Teacher Learning Centre Checklist
BL	17	Teacher Learning Centre Checklist
BL	18	Teacher Planning Sheet
BL	19	Teacher Long-range Planning Sheet
BL	20	Teacher Observation Sheet
BL	21	Teacher Observation Summary Sheet
BL	22	Teacher Checklist for Completed Activities
BL	23	Teacher Checklist for Writing
BL	24	Teacher Writing Conference Sheet
BL	25	Teacher Parent/Guardian Interview Checklist

Sample Letters to Parents/Guardians

BL	26 - BL 32	Parent/Guardian Letters

Blackline Masters

For Student Use

*To be photocopied or adapted
and modified to meet your
students' individual needs*

EVALUATE YOUR GROUP WORK

Name _____

Date _____

Group Members' Names _____

_____

_____

_____

_____

Check the statements that apply to you.

1. I listened to others while they were speaking. ☐

2. I offered my own ideas and information. ☐

3. I asked others for their ideas. ☐

4. I shared the materials and supplies. ☐

5. I asked my group for help when I needed it. ☐

6. I helped someone in my group. ☐

7. I took my turn and encouraged others to take their turns. ☐

8. I praised someone in the group. ☐

WORKING TOGETHER

Did we share?   ☺ 😐 ☹

Did we take turns?   ☺ 😐 ☹

Did we say something nice to each other?   ☺ 😐 ☹

Did we help each other?   ☺ 😐 ☹

WORKING TOGETHER

Did we share?   ☺ 😐 ☹

Did we take turns?   ☺ 😐 ☹

Did we say something nice to each other?   ☺ 😐 ☹

Did we help each other?   ☺ 😐 ☹

MY CONTRACT

I, _____ , will do my best to finish:

_____

_____

_____

_____

_____

by _____

                            (due date)

_____   _____

Student's Signature   *Teacher's Signature*

Comments _____

_____

_____

_____

_____

_____   _____

Student's   *Teacher's*
Initials   *Initials*

MY CONTRACT

What I *must* do today . . . _____

_____

_____

_____

What I *might* do today . . . _____

_____

_____

_____

_____   _____

Student's Signature   *Teacher's Signature*

MY CONTRACT

What I *must* do today . . . _____

_____

_____

_____

What I *might* do today . . . _____

_____

_____

_____

_____   _____

Student's Signature   *Teacher's Signature*

MY READING RECORD   Name _____

Date	Pages Read	Title	Comments

| | | MY WRITING RECORD SHEET   Name _____ | | | | | |

Date	Theme/Title of Writing	First Draft	Revised	Edited	Published	Teacher's Comment

PLANNING SHEET FOR THE WEEK OF _____

Name _____

	Monday	Tuesday	Wednesday	Thursday	Friday

MY TRACKING SHEET

Name _____

Centres	Date Started	Date Completed	Comments (Self-evaluation)
1.			
2.			
3.			
4.			
5.			
6.			

MY TRACKING SHEET

Name _____

Week of _____

MUSTS

WANTS

Name _____   Starting Date _____

MY ACTIVITY CHECKLIST

Stamp or print the date in the date column when you have completed an activity.

Activity ("Musts" are marked with an *.)	Date	My Comment	Teacher's Comment
1.			
2.			
3.			
4.			
5.			
6.			
7.			
8.			
9.			
10.			
11.			
12.			

KEEPING TRACK

Date _____   Name _____

What I Plan to Do _____

_____

_____

_____

_____

_____

What I Did _____

_____

_____

_____

_____

_____

_____

How I Felt_____

_____

_____

_____

Teacher's Comment _____

MY TRACKING SHEET   Name _____

Today's Date	Name of Centre	Description of Each Activity I Worked On or Completed	Comments

MY TRACKING SHEET

Name _____

Each column represents one centre completed. Fill in each box in the column before going on to your next centre.

	Centre	Centre	Centre
Name of Centre			
Date Started			
Describe the activity you chose.			
Date Completed			
What materials did you use for this activity?			
Who did you help, work or share with?			
Rate your results and circle.	Wow! Okay. Could be better.	Wow! Okay. Could be better.	Wow! Okay. Could be better.
Rate your effort and circle.	Wow! Okay. Could be better.	Wow! Okay. Could be better.	Wow! Okay. Could be better.
Did you clean up at your centre?			
Teacher's Comments			

Blackline Masters

For Teacher Use

*To be photocopied or adapted
and modified to meet your
students' individual needs*

What procedures do you have for student entry into the classroom?

_____

What are student tasks upon entry...
 — in the morning?

_____

 — after recess?

_____

 — after lunch?

_____

 — after physical education?

_____

 — other?

_____

What are your expectations for students...
 — in large group situations?

_____

 — in small group activities?

_____

 — for individual activities?

_____

 — for indoor recess?

_____

What do your students do upon task completion?

_____

What are your washroom exit and entry procedures?

_____

What procedures do you have for storage of...
 — students' personal belongings?

_____

. . . / 2

. . . / 2

— students' work?

_____

— group or class materials and resources?

_____

— teacher resources?

_____

How do you distribute materials to students?

_____

How do you collect student material?

_____

What are your procedures for exit and entry for fire drill, gym, library, other?

_____

What procedures do you have for clean-up?
(individual/group responsibilities, monitors)

_____

How do you distribute materials to go home with students?

_____

What are your procedures for student dismissal?

_____

What other routines and expectations have you established to encourage appropriate behaviour?

_____

_____

_____

_____

_____

_____

LEARNING CENTRE CHECKLIST

Things to Do for the _____ Centre

Materials to Collect		Materials to Prepare
Equipment	**Manipulative Materials**	
☐	☐	☐ signs for centres
☐	☐	☐ task cards
☐	☐	☐ student worksheets
☐	☐	☐ games
☐	☐	☐ students' folders/scrapbooks
☐	☐	☐
☐	☐	☐
☐	☐	☐
☐	☐	☐
Student Resources		**Other**
☐		
☐		
☐		
☐		
☐		
☐		
☐		
☐		

LEARNING CENTRE CHECKLIST

Name of Centre	Activities at Centre	Materials Needed

LEARNING CENTRE CHECKLIST

Does this active learning situation/centre provide:

☐ signs and labels?

☐ clear instructions (oral and written)?

☐ concrete manipulative materials?

☐ materials easily accessible to the students?

☐ storage and display areas for materials, resources and student work?

☐ opportunities for active learning —
"experiencing, interacting, reflecting and communicating"?

☐ tasks at varying levels of ability?

☐ open-ended tasks (no "right" answers)?

☐ student choice of tasks?

☐ opportunities for problem solving and risk taking?

☐ co-operative group learning experiences?

☐ a balance between large group, small group and individual activities?

☐ opportunities for student evaluation and peer evaluation?

BALANCING LARGE GROUP, SMALL GROUP AND INDIVIDUAL EXPERIENCES

Title _____

Small Group

Individual

Large Group

Curriculum Areas	Content Areas		Fall	Winter	Summer
Communications	Mathematics	Number			
		Measurement			
		Geometry			
	Language — Listening, Speaking, Reading, Writing, Viewing, Dramatizing				
The Arts	Dramatic Arts				
	Visual Arts				
	Music				
	Physical Education/Health				
Environmental Studies	Science				
	Social Studies				

OBSERVATION SHEET

STUDENT SUMMARY SHEET

Name _____	Fall, Winter or Spring Term

Social and Emotional Development	Work Habits

Language	Mathematics

Drama	Visual Arts	Music	Physical Education/ Health Education

Social Studies	Science

French	Computer

CHECKLIST FOR COMPLETED ACTIVITIES

Names of Students	Centres								Comments

OBSERVING CHILDREN'S WRITING

CONTENT

Type of Writing
- [ ] Expressive
- [ ] Transactional
- [ ] Poetic

Maturity
- [ ] Egocentric
- [ ] Bed-to-bed pattern
- [ ] Awareness of others
- [ ] Awareness of audience

Development of Story Line
- [ ] A beginning
- [ ] A middle
- [ ] An ending
- [ ] Sufficient information
- [ ] Well developed
- [ ] Unity of thought
- [ ] Smooth flow of ideas

Organization
- [ ] Coherent
- [ ] Logical
- [ ] Sequential
- [ ] Suits the purpose of the writing

Language
- [ ] Appropriate to the writing
- [ ] Use of descriptive words
- [ ] Use of conversation
- [ ] Use of metaphors
- [ ] Use of similes

Interest
- [ ] Holds audience's attention
- [ ] Imaginative
- [ ] Humorous
- [ ] Repetition for effect

MECHANICS

Grammar and Usage
- [ ] Sentence fragments
- [ ] Complete sentences
- [ ] Run-on sentences
- [ ] Short sentences
- [ ] Subject-verb agreement
- [ ] Use of conjunctions
- [ ] Use of adjectives
- [ ] Use of adverbs
- [ ] Use of clauses
- [ ] Use of adverbial clauses

Capitalization
- [ ] Beginning of sentences
- [ ] Proper names

Punctuation
- [ ] Use of periods
- [ ] Use of question marks
- [ ] Use of exclamation marks
- [ ] Use of quotation marks
- [ ] Use of commas

Spelling
- [ ] Use of scribble
- [ ] Use of random letters
- [ ] Use of initial consonants
- [ ] Use of phonetic spelling
- [ ] Use of conventional spelling with few errors
- [ ] Use of plurals
- [ ] Use of endings (-ed, -ing, -tion)

WRITING CONFERENCE SHEET

Name _____   Date _____

Type of Writing _____
                           (expressive, transactional, poetic)

Subject of Writing_____

Type of Conference _____
                       (choosing a topic, storytelling, drafting, revising, editing, publishing)

Issues Discussed _____

Follow-up_____

_____

_____

WRITING CONFERENCE SHEET

Name _____   Date _____

Type of Writing _____
                            (expressive, transactional, poetic)

Subject of Writing_____

Type of Conference _____
                       (choosing a topic, storytelling, drafting, revising, editing, publishing)

Issues Discussed _____

Follow-up_____

_____

_____

A CHECKLIST FOR SUCCESSFUL PARENT/GUARDIAN INTERVIEWS

☐ **Be Prepared to Discuss:**
- Purpose of interview
- Key issues
- Student Work Samples
- Records
- Background information
- Suggestions for parents

☐ **Start and Finish on Time**

☐ **Be Positive**
- Focus on strengths
- Work as a team with parents

☐ **Be Encouraging**
- Praise when appropriate

☐ **Be an Active Listener**

☐ **Be Confident**

☐ **Be Professional and Avoid Discussing**
- Other children
- Experiences with other teachers
- Other teachers' programs

☐ **Show Appreciation to Parents**
- For being present
- For being interested
- For being involved

☐ **Be Yourself!**

Blackline Masters

Sample Letters to Parents/Guardians

*To be photocopied or adapted
and modified to meet your
students' individual needs*

Dear Parent or Guardian

For our first social studies unit this term, our class will
be involved in a study of _____.
The children will be investigating _____
_____
_____.

This study will develop and strengthen the skills of_____
_____
_____.

Thank you for your continuing interest and support.

Sincerely

Dear Parent or Guardian

Our class has completed an environmental studies unit on
_____. This
unit illustrated to the children that _____
_____
_____.

It involved activities such as _____
_____
_____.

The children enjoyed taking part in this unit of study and
are looking forward to sharing their work with you at this
time.

Sincerely

Dear Parent or Guardian

Throughout the school year, your child may mention his/her involvement in "learning centres".

In our classroom, "learning centres" are planned around various themes or curriculum areas. These centres encourage the developing physical, social, emotional and intellectual needs of the children. When taking part in these centres, your child will have many opportunities to work with a group, to develop and strengthen the understanding of concepts and skills, to make decisions, and to solve problems.

Interaction with their fellow students and between teacher and students at centres promotes co-operation--an essential life skill--and makes for valuable and positive learning experiences.

Attached to this letter is a list of the centres that your child will be taking part in this term.

If you have any questions, please call me at the school at _____.

Sincerely

Dear Parent or Guardian

I would like to outline some of the language learning experiences that your child will have this year.

SPEAKING

There will be daily opportunities for your child to express questions, ideas and opinions, in large group discussions, with a partner, and with adults. These opportunities are designed to encourage communication skills.

LISTENING

Listening carefully is an important part of our language program. Children must learn to listen carefully in order to learn new facts and ideas and to understand instructions and directions. Development of listening skills will be emphasized in large and small group discussions, and also at our audio-visual centre.

READING

Research has proven that children learn to read by reading. The more they read and discuss what they read, the better readers they will become. Our focus is to encourage children to read for meaning, to understand what they are reading and to read more fluently. To reach this goal, the children will take part in many reading activities throughout the day.

I hope that you will encourage your child to read at home and that you or another adult will read to her/him daily.

WRITING

The writing program this year emphasizes daily writing and a sense of authorship. The children will be involved in much the same activities as real authors. They will

- discuss their ideas
- talk out their stories
- write draft copies
- share their stories
- change and revise/rework selected stories
- edit and publish selected stories

..../2

Page 2

When the children first write their stories, I encourage them to write all the letters they hear and not to worry about correct spelling at first. In this way, their thoughts will flow freely onto paper. The students will be revising or changing selected pieces of their writing. When they prepare to share their work with others, they see the need for correct spelling, punctuation and grammar. When they publish their writing, they gain confidence and pride in their accomplishments.

I hope that you will encourage your child to write often at home. I would welcome sharing any home writing at school.

SPELLING

The children's spelling skills will improve as they read, write and experiment with words. Research has shown that children must feel free to try different spellings before they become competent spellers. They will be working with words from their own writing and from their theme studies.

MUSIC

The music program will also emphasize language. Children read and learn new words to a variety of new songs and sing for enjoyment. The music program will also involve experimenting with sound, rhythm, and movement.

I hope to communicate with you frequently. Please get in touch with me if you have any questions or concerns. Call the school at _____.

Sincerely

Dear Parent or Guardian

The following suggestions are some practical ideas for you to use to encourage your child to read at home.

- Set up a shelf with his/her favourite books.
- Make regular trips to the library.
- Ask the librarian to recommend good books.
- Give books as gifts.
- Let your child see you read. Children learn by imitating.
- Read and share books and stories with your child regularly in the language you are most comfortable with.
- Establish a regular daily reading time, for example, after supper or before bedtime.
- Relate reading to everyday life situations (billboards, traffic signs, menus, TV guides, catalogues, labels, maps, etc.)

Thank you for your continuing interest and support.

Sincerely

Dear Parent or Guardian

As you know, learning to write effectively is a very important part of your child's education. Here are some practical ideas on how you can help your child with writing at home.

. Let your child see you write often. Show that writing is a purposeful, real-life activity.

. Leave your child notes (in lunch boxes, under pillows) and encourage her/him to write back.

. Encourage your child to help in writing out shopping lists, birthday cards, invitations, etc.

. Purchase a diary and suggest that your child make daily entries.

. Encourage your child to write letters. Help him/her find a pen pal.

. Have paper, pencils, markers, etc., available to encourage writing at home.

. Find a place in your home for writing or doing school work.

. Whenever possible, take your child on outings such as to shopping malls, museums, planetariums, art displays, concerts, sporting events, an airport, a farm, city hall, a zoo, amusement parks, and family vacations. These enriching experiences will be possible topics for your child's writing.

. Discuss possible ideas for writing with your child.

. Be an audience for your child's ideas.

Thank you for your continuing interest and support.

Sincerely

Dear Parent or Guardian

Here are some practical suggestions on how you can help your child do well in school and enjoy learning.

- Let your child explore and experiment with materials, toys and "hands-on" activities such as building with blocks, typing, cooking and sewing. Children learn best by <u>doing</u>.

- Take advantage of daily learning situations to point out colours, numbers, letters and words. Count the number of plates on the table, talk about the colours in the striped shirt he/she is wearing, read and discuss prices during shopping outings.

- Oversee the type of television programs your child watches and control how much time she/he spends watching. Discuss the programs with your child and make television a shared experience.

- Let your child be responsible for some household chore.

- Let your child make decisions by giving him/her choice in such matters as breakfast food, birthday celebrations, bedroom colour, clothing, etc.

- Seek out your child's strengths and capabilities and praise her/him whenever possible.

- Play games with your child that require concentration. Often such games can help to increase problem-solving and thinking skills.

- Have good conversations with your child and ask thought-provoking questions. Listen actively.

Thank you for your continuing interest and support.

Sincerely